Adams Central
Art Dept.
1976

DESIGN

FOR ARTISTS AND CRAFTSMEN

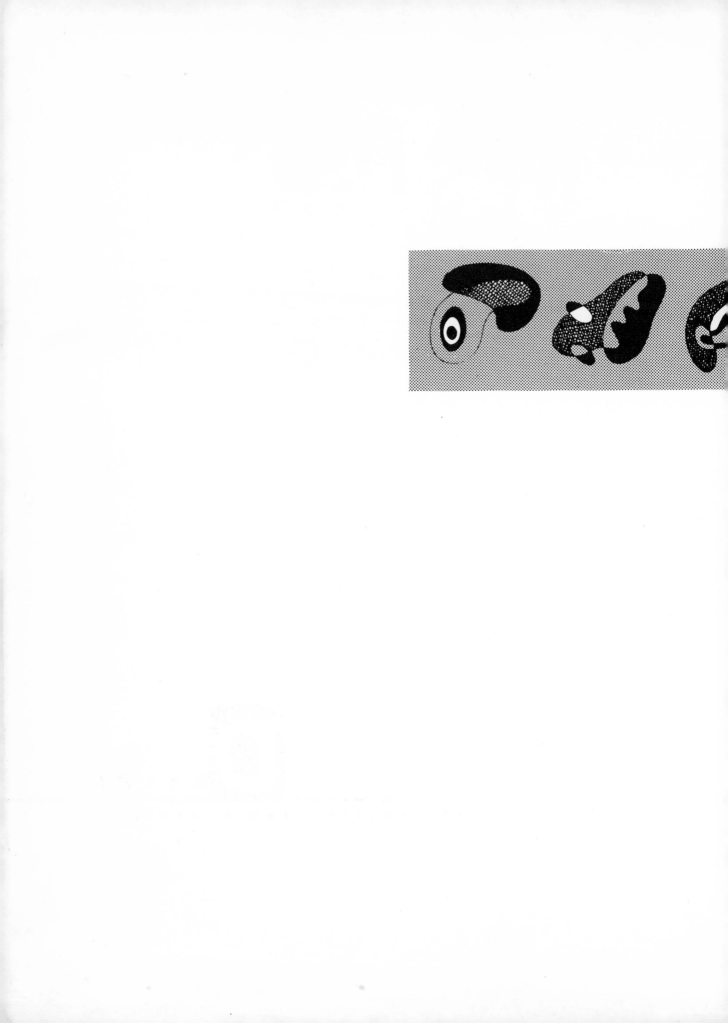

DESIGN

for artists and craftsmen

LOUIS WOLCHONOK

DOVER PUBLICATIONS, INC.

NEW YORK

Published in Canada by General Publishing Company, Ltd.,
30 Lesmill Road, Don Mills, Toronto, Ontario.

Published in the United Kingdom by Constable and Company, Ltd.,
10 Orange Street, London W.C. 2.

Design for Artists and Craftsmen is a new work, first
published by Dover Publications, Inc., in 1953.

Standard Book Number: 486-20274-7
Library of Congress Catalog Card Number: 54-9269

Manufactured in the United States of America

Dover Publications, Inc.
180 Varick Street
New York, N.Y. 10014

DEDICATION

To my wife, without whom this book would not be possible.

ACKNOWLEDGMENT

I owe a debt of gratitude to many of my former students. I doubt whether they learned more from me than I did from them.

Many thanks to my friends, Alexander Lindey and Harold V. Walsh, for their interest and wise counsel.

CONTENTS

FOREWORD

Suppose that you had in front of you a diverse group of art objects consisting of a Greek vase, a painting on silk by a Chinese master, a Flemish tapestry, easel paintings by a Dutch master and by a great figure in contemporary art, and finally, a piece of sculpture by a Peruvian craftsman.

In a general way, the subject matter in this interesting collection might very well include a three-dimensional geometric shape, human figures dressed as warriors, mountains, plants, tigers, a purely imaginative creature (the unicorn), an interior depicting a drinking scene, a combination of geometric figures, and an ingeniously designed serpent.

There would be startling differences in the styles, degrees of simplification of the forms used, and the emotional content expressed in these works. There would be many good reasons for the differences, but what is perhaps more startling than anything else is the fact that even though the span of time represented extends over a period of twenty-five hundred years in widely separated countries and civilizations, there would be two common factors. The first would be the compelling urge to create, and the second would be the essential sameness of the basic forms from which the masterpieces were created. It is with the second common factor that I am particularly concerned in this book.

The basic forms are geometric, flower and plant, animal, human, and man-made. From time immemorial they have been used with never-ending variety and a wealth of imagination and ingenuity. It is no less true today that the basic material is the same as it always was and as it will be in the predictable future. It becomes clear that the artist, the designer, the craftsman, must become intimately acquainted with the material common to everyone and at everyone's disposal. Obviously, copying somebody else's work or permitting a mechanical device, such as a camera, to take the place of direct contact and experience is at best a poor substitute, and it has never resulted nor will ever result in the creation of any art product which will stand the test of time.

A good way to start is to put down on paper the things you like and the things you like to do. Suppose, merely for the purpose of illustration, you choose dancing as something you like to watch. Your interest in dancing may become a subject for expression in color, wood, or metal. Let us suppose further that you have had little or no experience in drawing the human figure. What then? Is the lack of such training to be a hindrance to all the enjoyment to be derived from using subject matter in which you have a special interest? It need not. The essential thing is to do it anyway. It will turn out to be crude, childish, even silly, and you may become the butt of a few jokes about your work, but the inescapable result will be that you have made a start. You will have done something that will open your eyes to the fact that the ability to express yourself in an art form requires observation, memory training, perseverance, courage, elimination of preconceived notions, and an active attitude towards experimentation. Above everything else, don't be misled into thinking that you can learn to draw, paint, sculpt, or anything else in a few easy lessons, and that before you know it, you will be a master-craftsman. Giving adequate and satisfying expression to your ideas is not easy and takes time and effort, but it is exciting, exhilarating and will give you a sense of fulfillment that will more than compensate for all the hardships.

Your aim should be to perfect yourself to the ultimate limit of your ability. No one of us knows when that point is reached. That is why participation in creative art is so absorbing and why you have every right to look forward to the next thing that you do as being the best one. If the newest work does not meet with your complete satisfaction, and it seldom does, keep on working.

I may be accused of over-simplification and indifference to the frustrations and disappointments that do appear, but in justification of my point of view, there is a background of many years of experience as a teacher and professional painter, designer, and craftsman.

Don't infer from any remark in this brief statement or in the book itself that, after study-ing my methods in design and composition, you will be able to turn out impressive work. Strange as it may seem, I am not interested in whether your work or the work of my students, with whom I am in personal contact, turns out to be good or bad. The one chief thing that does interest and concern me is to be of assistance in getting you to do the best that you can possibly do.

I suggest that you draw every day, both from actual objects and from memory, even if you can spare only a few minutes.

Until you are well advanced, do not use photographs to get your material. If you do use them, employ them only to augment your knowledge gained from direct observation and practice, not as a substitute for it.

Do the exercises suggested in the text. Whenever possible, use your own source material.

It is not necessary to proceed with a study of the text in the order in which the various chapters are presented. Go to the parts that interest you most, but do not neglect the subject matter of lesser interest.

Pay close attention to the chapter on geometric form because it introduces the funda-mental lines, surfaces, and solids that are the bases of all design.

Design involves control and a knowledge of the function of the tools that are used in its creation, but it is also much more than that. It is a living thing that grows out of the hopes, the dreams, the longings, and the aspirations of human beings. The animated, lively, living thing that is design cannot be described in words, nor can it be taught.

SECTION ONE

GEOMETRIC FORM

INTRODUCTION

Most people think that geometric figures are so foreign to them that they shy away from them. As soon as anything remotely connected with geometry is mentioned, it generally brings back unpleasant memories of difficulties encountered in student days. As a result, it is taken for granted that any kind of design based on the properties of mathematical figures will be difficult, if not impossible, to master. Such an attitude is unfortunate, even if understandable, because it shuts out a wealth of material for the designer that is not only comparatively easy to handle but offers a wide field for self-expression.

Some of the geometric figures used as basic material in this chapter are the line, triangle, rectangle, circle, plane and rounded surfaces, and solids. Perhaps you aren't conscious of it, but in your every-day living you have occasion to see many of the figures mentioned. It would be a very strange world indeed if they were not present. Consider a line first. The extreme edges of this sheet of paper are lines. The intersection between a wall and a floor of the room in which you are sitting is a line. A rectangular box, such as a Uneeda Biscuit box, has many lines in it. If you ask yourself what other common objects have lines in them that can be readily seen, you will be astonished at the vast number that you will be able to name. If you go on to inspect all the objects around you that you see and use in your daily living, you will discover that a can of beans has a circular top and bottom and that the lateral surface is cylindrical. The fruit you eat may be an orange which is almost spherical; the lampshade on your desk may be conical, etc. etc.

I should like to make a distinction between the geometric figures that we encounter in our daily living and the abstract geometric figures of the world of mathematics.

Man-made things are imperfect, relatively speaking, precisely because they are man-made. The straight line that is a corner of the room is not perfectly straight. The surfaces of a box are not absolutely smooth. The line we draw on a sheet of paper has some thickness; therefore, it cannot be a line in the mathematical sense. While the differences between the abstract entities and the actual objects are many, we need not be bothered by this fact, especially since the designer has to be an inventor and a person with imagination. If the designer is all of these things, he uses the geometric forms for his own purposes and doesn't worry about the mathematics involved. Even if you hated mathematics in your student days, you can still learn to use geometric figures to your great advantage.

Motion plays a very important role in understanding the nature of geometric figures.

A moving point generates a line, whether straight or curved.

A moving line sweeps out a surface.

A moving surface forms a solid.

Try to picture in your mind's eye how the various figures are created, and you will become aware of the dynamic nature of geometry. It is indeed a very fruitful source of inspiration for the designer.

PLATE 1. Row A shows straight lines and open and closed figures, combining straight lines.

Row C shows curved lines and open and closed figures, combining curved lines.

Row B shows combinations of straight and curved lines.

EXERCISE 1: Invent different combinations, using the same set of figures.

EXAMPLE:

Figure 1, Row B.

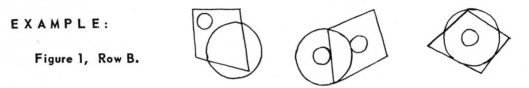

EXERCISE 2:   (a) Take from combined figures several simple combinations of lines. (Figure 2, Row B).

(b) By repetition, create running patterns.

(c) Repeat, using axis of symmetry.

Fig. 2, Row B,

Example (a).

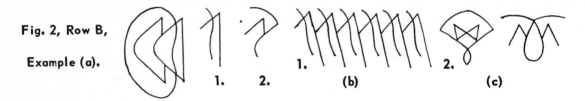

EXERCISE 3: Repetition of same shape. Variations in size and position.

EXAMPLE: Semi-circle.

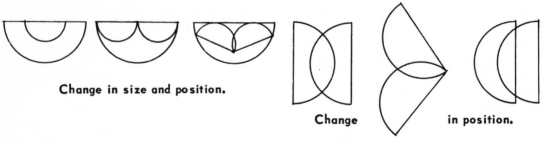

Change in size and position.

Change   in position.

EXERCISE 4: Invention of closed, irregular figures:

(1) All straight lines.

(2) Straight and curved lines.

(3) All curved lines.

EXAMPLE:

1.   2.   3.

EXERCISE 5: Invent combinations of closed, irregular figures.

EXAMPLE:

A.   B.   C.

PLATE 1

P L A T E   2.   A line, whether straight or curved, is the result of the successive positions of a point moving in a definite way. For example, a straight line is generated when the direction of the moving point remains the same. A circle is formed when a point moves so that every position is equidistant from a point within.

The line that is nothing more than a scribble cannot be defined, even though segments of it may be circular or elliptical.

I am making a distinction between what is called a mathematical and a non-mathematical line. The scribble, the automatic, and the non-mathematical line must not be dismissed, because they may serve useful purposes in design.

Most of the lines in Plate 2, while neither automatic nor scribbles, are non-mathematical, yet they have a rhythmic order which suggests control. They are design lines, as distinguished from mathematical lines.

Think of the space enclosed by three straight lines. Ordinarily, we call such a figure a triangle. The triangle, or any other closed space, represents not only a special kind of area but a line or series of lines which result from a definite movement of a point.

If we think in terms of motion, the line takes on a dynamic quality, and the figure, of which the line is a part, shares in the dynamism.

Note that in all of the definitions of geometric figures, two and three-dimensional, the manner in which they were generated has been stressed. The figures came into being as a result of motion.

It is the element of motion that I am emphasizing.

Motion may also be induced by the proper juxtaposition of color and values.

If is quite possible that the motion inherent in line and color is the unique property of design which distinguishes it from other forms of expression.

In Plate 2, think of each figure as the path of a moving point. All of the figures are open. To create a closed figure, all that you need to do is to make the moving point return to its original position. The total shape which represents the complete path of the moving point may resemble common figures, such as triangles, rectangles, circles. Sometimes the line formed takes on the appearance of the head of an animal. In fact, there is no limit to the diverse fantasies that can be invented.

E X E R C I S E 1:
Create a series of open figures using combinations of straight and curved lines. (Have a contour in mind, such as a triangle, rectangle, circle, etc.).

E X E R C I S E 2:
Combine open figures.

E X E R C I S E   3: Create a series of closed figures of three or more sides, using combinations of all straight, straight and curved, or all curved lines.

N O T E : Start at a fixed point A. Go as far as you wish, then stop, change direction, but do not retrace your steps. This gives a feeling of continuity to the motion.

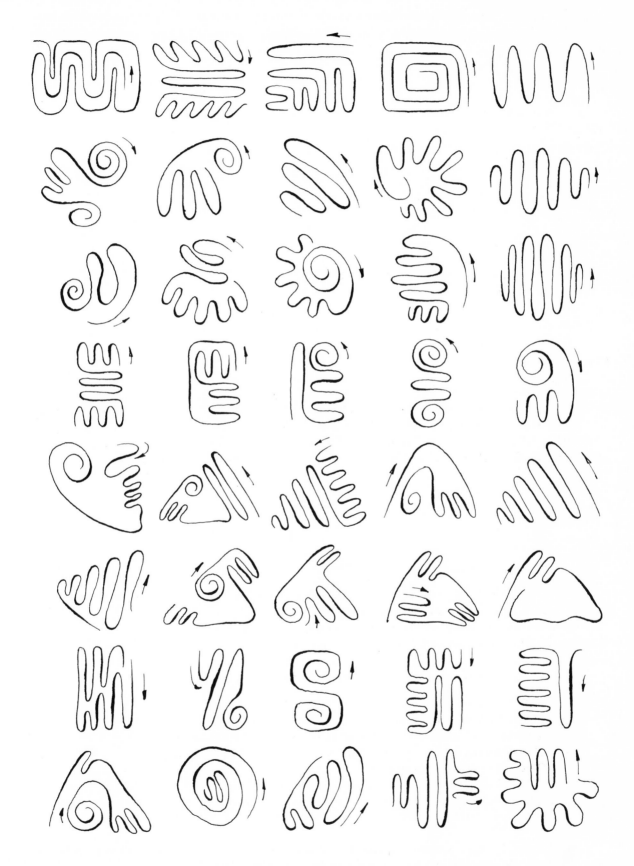

PLATE 2

P L A T E   3 .   Free-form figures.

A two-dimensional free form is a closed plane figure whose contour is a continuously flowing line in which there are no intersecting segments.

A.

The following are <u>not</u> free forms:

B.

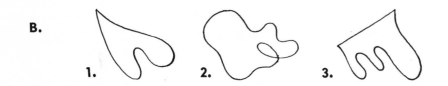

In figure B, number 1 shows a point of stoppage. The movement of the eye is arrested. (This is called a cusp).

2 shows a point of stoppage which also arrests the movement of the eye. (This is called a node).

3, using a straight line, immediately gives us at least two points at which the eye stops. The plane free form may be considered a derivative of the circle.

If we think of a circle as being made of a substance which retains its new shape each time part of the circle is stretched or indented, then we can envision the transformation.

When free forms are intersected, the character of the free form is altered to some degree because points of stoppage are introduced.

If there are too many points of intersection, confusion may result; first, because of the many points of interest; second, because too many unrelated small areas may disturb the composition.

Plate 3 shows a series of designs in which various free forms have been combined.

1.   A, B, and G have two basic figures.

2.   The elaborations in A and B are produced by repeat lines. In G, the two figures intersect and the chief interest is contained in the part formed by the intersection.

3.   The remaining designs are combinations of three or more free forms.

4.   Figure G resembles a butterfly.

5.   Figure F in part resembles a human face. You will find that as you work with geometric figures, many of the designs will take on the appearance of natural forms. Very often, the artist does it intentionally, but it also happens that the effect may be accidental.

E X E R C I S E :   Create a series of free forms and then combine in units of two, three, four, and five. Be sure that each has a definite area of chief interest.

A

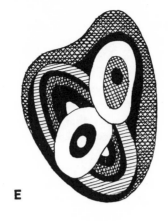

E

B

F

J

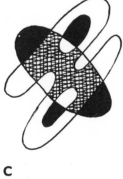

C

G

K

D

H

L

PLATE 3

PLATE 4. A designer is an inventor. He is always trying to imagine new combinations of shapes and colors. As you can see from what has already been presented in this chapter, geometrical figures offer lots of tools for his use.

One of the most important tools is the line.

In Plate 4, the line is used in two ways:

(1) It forms a connection between two elements (transition line);
(2) It forms a boundary that gives a definite character to a figure.

In each illustration, we start with two non-parallel straight lines. The problem is to join the two lines by a third line so that:

(A) The feeling of movement is increased.
(B) New areas are created to give added interest.

Choose a random point on one of the two already established lines. As the point moves from the line, it creates another line. The line thus created will be one of an astonishing number of possible connections. The types of space created will depend on the character of the line generated by the moving point.

In this plate, each drawing shows the path of a point as it moves from one line to another.

Figures 4 and 8 show the path of a point as it moves from one line to another and then returns to the first line.

Figures 13, 14, 15, and 16 show enveloping lines producing a closed space.

Figures 13 and 15 show that the enveloping line is independent of the figure produced by the moving point.

Figure 16, the enveloping line incorporates part of the point-moving line.

The sense of movement is heightened by the use of light and dark.

Each variation has been treated as a composition and has an area of chief interest.

EXERCISES: Draw the path of a point, joining two parallel line.

Draw the path of a point, joining a curved and a straight line.

In each exercise show:

(A) A series of open arrangements.
(B) A series of closed arrangements.
(C) An area of chief interest.

NOTE: The path of the moving point need not be curved — Figure 6.

1.

2.

3.

4.

5.

6.

7.

8.

9.

10.

11.

12.

13.

14.

15.

16.

PLATE 4

P L A T E   5.   We know that a straight line does not change its direction, no matter how long it is. In a curved line, however, the direction is constantly changing. The way to tell what the direction is at any point on the curve is to draw a straight line that touches the curve only at the chosen point. The direction of the straight line becomes the direction of the curve at the point. If a second and a third point on the curve are selected, the straight lines touching the curve at these points will indicate new directions.   (Fig. 3.)

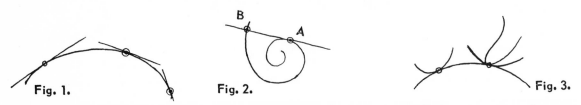

Fig. 1.   Fig. 2.   Fig. 3.

The straight line which touches the curve at one point is called a tangent to the curve at that point.

If the curve is a spiral, the straight line or tangent, if long enough, will intersect the curve.

In Figure 2, the straight line is tangent to the spiral only at Point A, because it is only at Point A that we now know the direction of the curve. Notice how the line cuts the spiral at another Point B on the curve, but at Point B, the direction of the curve is not indicated. Therefore, the straight line is not considered to be a tangent at Point B.

Now consider the following case: We can draw a curved line that will touch a given curve at one point only. (Fig. 3)

The curved line that we draw will not be a tangent because it will not indicate the direction of the curve.

N O T E :   Only one tangent can be drawn to a curve at a single point. (Fig.1) Any number of curved lines can be drawn to a curve that will touch the curve at a single point. (Fig.3)

In plate 5, the basic figure is a spiral. (A watch spring is a spiral. Many seashells have spirals in them).

The spiral, Fig. 4, is an open curve, growing ever larger as the moving point continues to generate the curve. (The circle and the ellipse are closed curves. Fig. 5.)

Fig. 4   Fig. 5

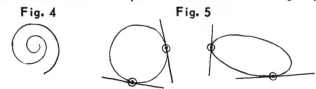

In Plate 5:

(1)   For the most part straight line tangents have been used to close the open spiral curve, and then repeat lines were added.

(2)   Each design, though very small, has an area of chief interest.

(3)   In the designs which have been numbered, curved lines are used instead of the tangent straight lines.

E X E R C I S E   (1) Create closed designs, using spiral as basic form by adding tangents and repeat lines.

(2)   Create closed designs, using two open curves by adding tangents and repeat lines.

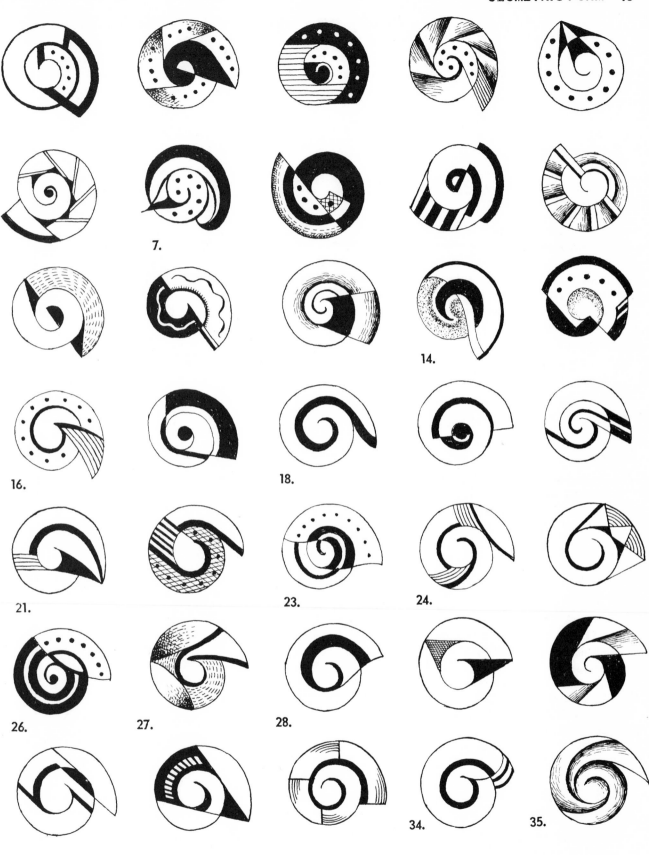

PLATE 5

PLATE 6. This plate represents a set of compositions in which triangles and circles are used in different combinations.

LINEAR ANALYSES OF DESIGNS IN PLATE 6

STEP 1. Sketchy outline in which the movement and positions of the principal parts are indicated.

STEP 2. Circles and triangles are added in places roughly indicated by sketchy lines.

STEP 3. The results of step 2 are checked to make sure that an area of chief interest is established.

STEP 4. Black and white values are added to complete the compositions. (Designs are checked to make sure that the black and white values do not detract from the center of interest.)

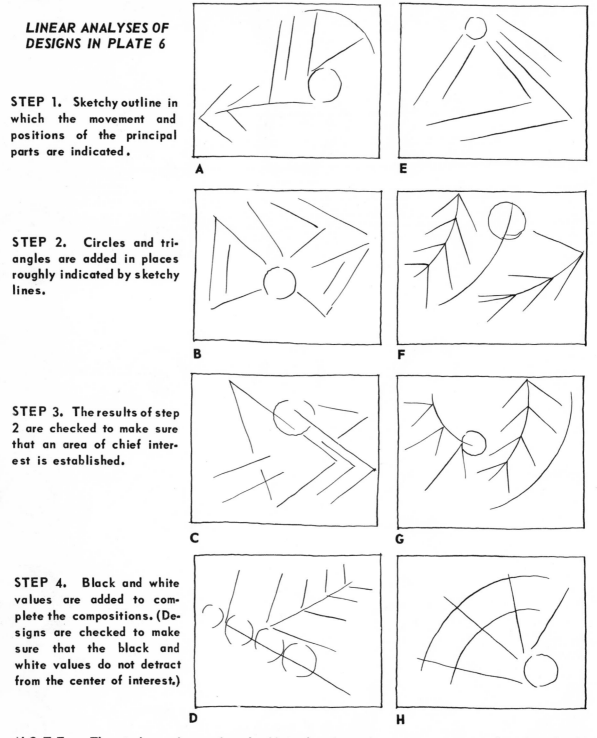

NOTE: The circles and triangles should not be of equal importance; one or the other should be dominant.

EXERCISES: Create compositions in frames of rectangles, squares, and circles, using the following combinations:

(1) All triangles; (2) Triangles and Rectangles; (3) Rectangles and Circles.

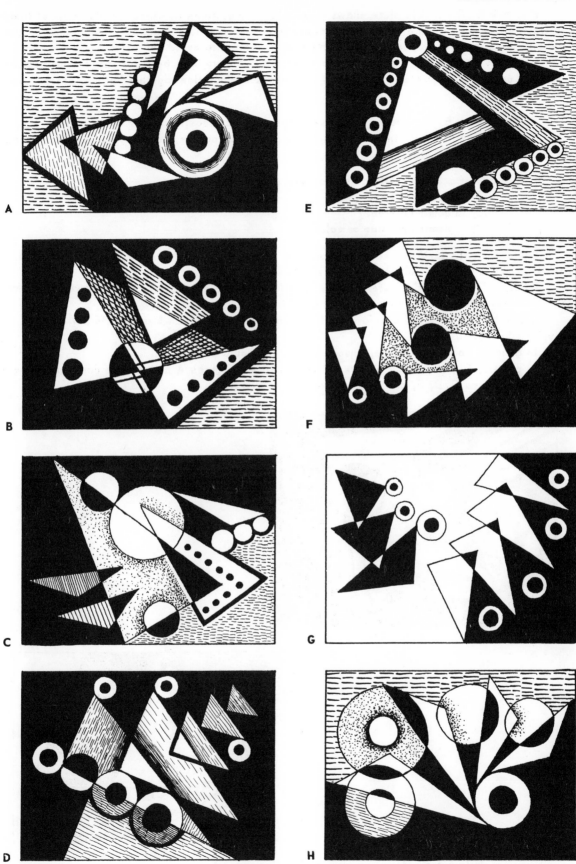

A

B

C

D

E

F

G

H

PLATE 6

P L A T E   7 :   This plate shows a group of compositions in which a wide range of lines and figures is used. When diverse elements are used, interest is immediately heightened by the different character of each part, but the parts must be united to avoid confusion.

When the same figure is repeated a great deal, the various parts of the design become somewhat uniform in character. This tends to hold the composition together but may create   too much monotony.

E X E R C I S E   1 :   Make layout sketches of the compositions in Plate 7.

E X E R C I S E   2 :   Invent original designs in rectangles, squares, and circles, based on diverse geometric figures.

N O T E : Each composition should have:
    (1) a dominant line.
    (2) a dominant area.
    (3) a dominant value or color.

DOMINANT LINE means emphasizing either the straight or the curved line. Very often it refers to the direction of the line as well.

DOMINANT AREA refers to the character of the spaces formed by curved lines or straight lines. It also refers to the area of chief interest.

DOMINANT VALUE refers to the various areas in which black, different degrees of grey, or white are used.

In general, sameness of line, shape, and value should be avoided.

In plate 7, Figures E and G have all curved lines; Figures A and B have dominant straight lines, and Figures C, D, F, and H have dominant curved lines.

A.

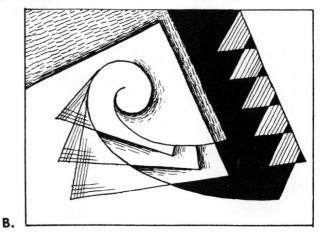

PLATE 7   B.

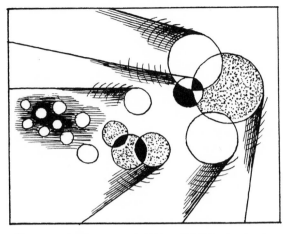

C

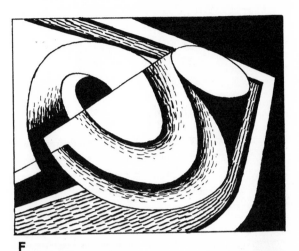

F

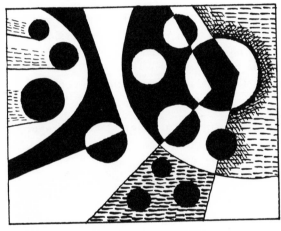

D

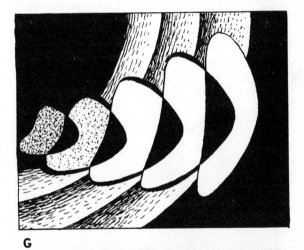

G

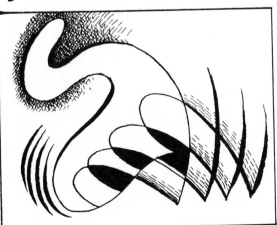

E

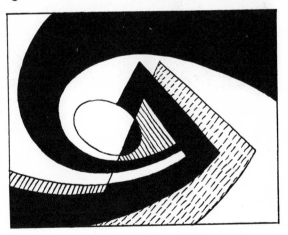

H

PLATE 7, *continued*

PLATE 8. This plate (Figures A, B, and C) shows how the same motif can be repeated in different ways to produce circular designs of great variety.

The motif used is Figure 1. It is constructed in the following way:

(1) Start with a square.

(2) Locate center of square, O, by two diagonals, AC and BD.

(3) Through center O, draw FG parallel to side BC.

(4) Through center O, draw EN parallel to side AB.

(5) Draw EF.

(6) With O as center, draw arc of circle with radius equal to OL. The arc will touch line FG at point J and point P.

(7) Point H is midway between points O and P.

(8) Draw line MK through point H, parallel to diagonal AC.

(9) Make arc of circle touch line MK at point R.

(10) Join points J and K.

If you examine Figures 2 and 3, you will be able to discover how these motifs were formed.

NOTE: Plate 10 is devoted to the invention of motifs from the basic square.

(1) Now return to Figures A, B, and C, and you will see how the chief interest has been controlled so that in Figure A, the middle part is emphasized; in Figure B, the outside is the most important; while in Figure C, the central part is of greatest interest.

(2) Repeat lines were used extensively in Figure C.

(3) Each point of the motif moves in a circle.   (The points rotate about the center of the circle).

EXERCISE: Using motifs in Figures 2 and 3, invent a series of circular designs.

EXAMPLE OF CHANGE OF EMPHASIS:

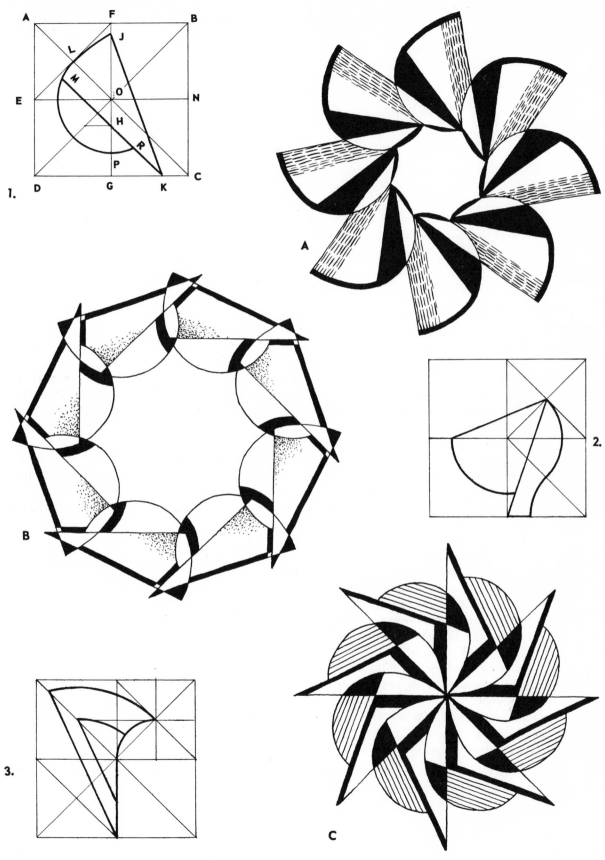

1.

A

B

2.

3.

C

PLATE 8

P L A T E   9 . The eight compositions are evolved from various combinations of the six geometric figures.

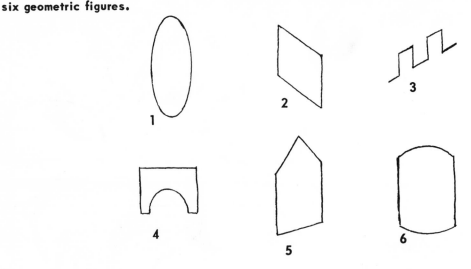

Figures A and B are quite realistic in comparison to the others.

The character of the design is a matter of choice and control. Choice represents your own tastes, desires, aspirations, while control involves your technical ability to use adequately the tools necessary to complete the design.

The arrangements represent the method of synthesis, the putting together of various elements to create a whole. The ideal way in which to achieve the whole is to get a crystal-clear picture of the entire composition in the mind's eye before actual work has begun. This is more easily said than done. It requires practice and discipline, and even the most experienced and talented designer doesn't always achieve it, but make it your goal.

It is especially important for anyone working three-dimensionally, to leave as little as possible to chance and the happy circumstance of good luck. It is easy to erase a pencil line or to paint over a surface, but to reshape a piece of metal, wood, or granite is quite a task. The more uncertainty in your mind, the more changing you will have to do, and in all probability, the final outcome will not represent the idea with which you started.

In fixing the idea in your mind, think of:

(1) The general over-all contours.

(2) The dominant lines (straight or curved).

(3) The dominant surfaces (plane or curved).

(4) The dominant solids (cubic or spherical).

(5) The area of chief interest.

(6) The less dominant areas.

(7) The mood of the whole.

The order in which you think of all of these things is not too important although I should think that the general over-all contours and volumes and mood would come first. The rest may be regarded as detail.

I do not pretend that the above list is complete, but there is enough in it to give you a very good working start.

It takes lots of doing, practice, and perseverance.

EXERCISE: Choose a group of motifs (not more than five or six), and create within given spaces a series of compositions. Remember, parts may be repeated, enlarged, changed in position, or omitted.

PLATE 9

PLATE   10.   Basic form is a square. Among its properties are equal sides and equal angles. Each angle is 90 degrees. From these facts arise many possible ways in which the figure can be divided.

Figs. 1 to 5 show how the complex figure is attained.

Figs. 6 to 10 show designs which have been abstracted from Fig. 5.

NOTE: In sub-dividing any figure:

(1)   A straight line can be drawn between any two points.

(2)   A straight line can be divided into any number of equal parts.

(3)   Through a fixed point, a line can be drawn parallel to a given line.

(4)   Through a fixed point, a line can be drawn perpendicular to a given line.

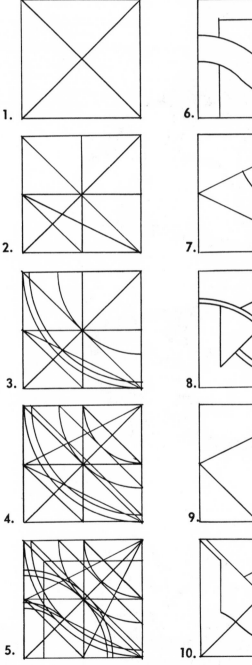

1.

2.

3.

4.

5.

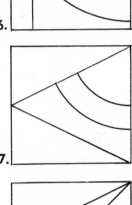

6.

7.

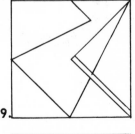

8.

9.

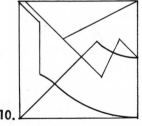

10.

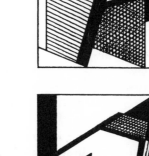

PLATE 10

P L A T E   11.   The basic form is the circle, and the general problem is that of using the properties of the circle as the basis for design.

Consider A and B: line 1-2 is the diameter; lines 0-1, 0-2, 0-3 are the radii.

As soon as we establish a fixed length for either the radius or the diameter of a circle, a great many relationships follow which are peculiar to the circle and to no other figure.

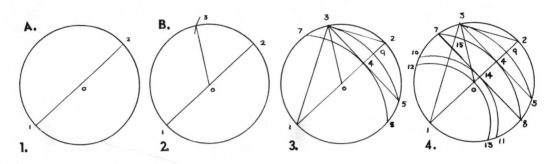

F I G U R E 1. Random diameter.

F I G U R E 2. With point 2 as center and radius equal to 0-2, locate point 3. Draw line 3-0.

F I G U R E 3. Draw lines 3-1, 3-2, 3-5 perpendicular to line 1-2. With point 1 as center and radius equal to 1-3, describe arc 3-9-5. Describe arc 7-4-8 with line 4-1 as radius.

F I G U R E 4. Draw line 7-8. Describe arc 10-14-11 with 1-14 as radius. Describe arc 12-0-13 with 1-0 as radius.

F I G U R E 5. Draw circle with center at 0 and radius equal to 0-4. Draw arc 16-15-17 with line 1-15 as radius. Draw lines 1-12, 1-10, 1-11, 1-8, 1-5, 1-15, 15-2, 2-18, 2-19.

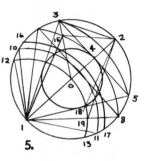

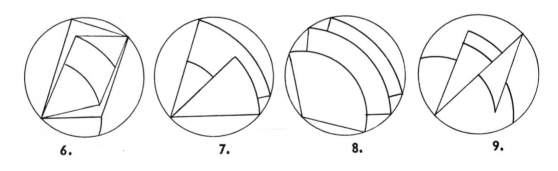

Figures 6-10 show five different combinations which have been abstracted from Figure 5.

The illustrations in Plate 11 show only a few of the many ways in which a circle can be divided.

Figures 6, 7, and 9 are asymmetric while figures 8 and 10 have in each instance an axis of symmetry.

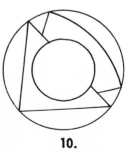

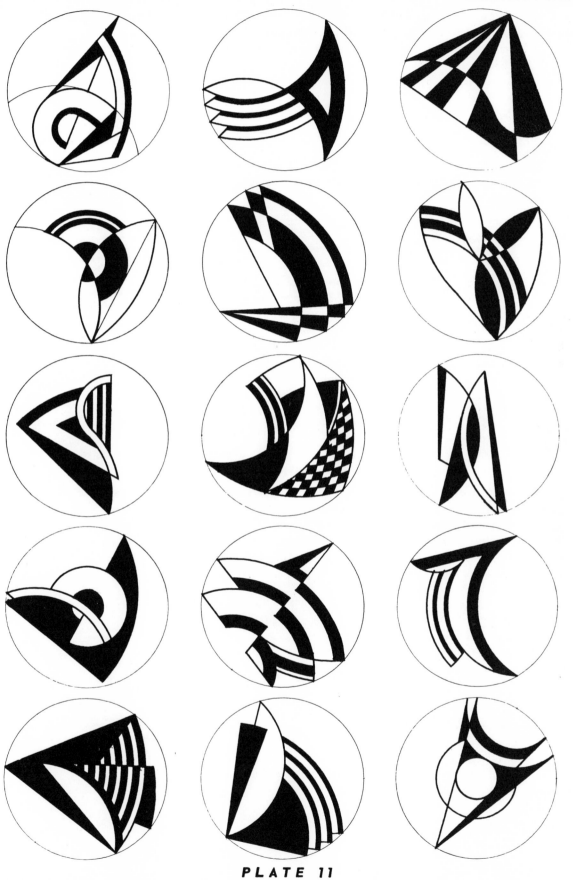

PLATE 11

P L A T E   12 .   Free form compositions.

In figures A, B, C, and D, I have used a modification of the free form.

Start with a free form such as

Figure 1:

Suppose that it were cut out of paper and then one end of it were lifted. We should still have the free form but it would no longer be wholly two-dimensional. It would become a space form or three-dimensional.

Figure 2:

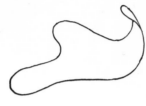

Figure 3 :

E X E R C I S E :   Create a series of compositions using the free form and its variants in pre-determined spaces:

(1)   Composition based on intersecting diagonals (Figures E and H).
(2)   Composition based on radiation (Figure A).

Figures 2 and 3 on this page may be interpreted in two ways: First, as modified free-form figures; second, as projections or representations of three-dimensional free-form figures.

If the second interpretation is considered, one view as shown is not enough to give an unmistakable picture of the space figure. This is important to the designer who is thinking in three dimensions. He should show by a sufficient number of drawings of different aspects of the object the complete whole and leave no room for misinterpretation.

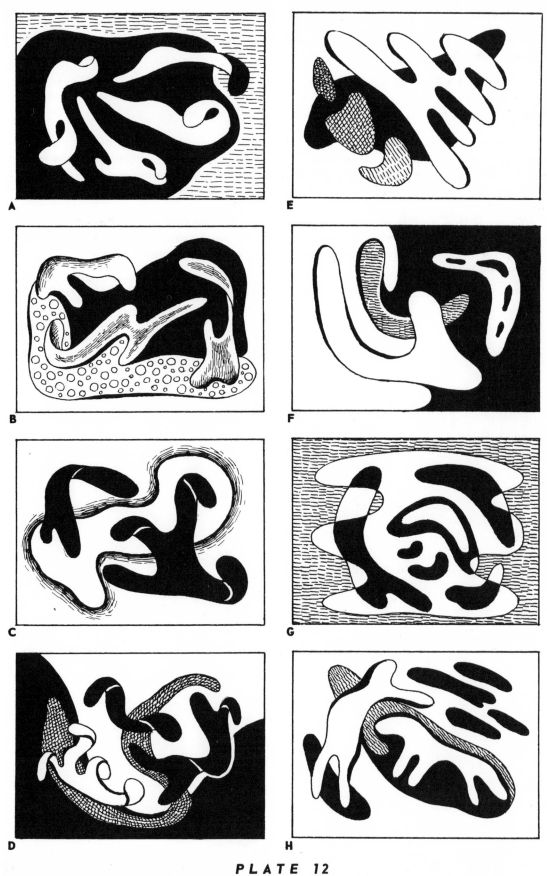

PLATE 12

P L A T E 1 3 . Abstract composition based on geometric form.

E X E R C I S E : Separate the various geometric figures that are used and then recombine them to form new compositions.

E X E R C I S E : Combine various geometric figures of your own invention to form complete arrangements.

Allow figures to intersect (if you think necessary).

I have called the arrangement in Plate 13 an abstract composition. I dare say that no two readers will react to it in the same way. The motifs are purely geometric, but the manner in which they have been put together, the selection of light and dark areas, and the various concentrations of interests, will stimulate the eye and the mind to find many different meanings in the picture.

To me it is a work based upon my reactions to a movement from a Bach motet that I had studied. Whatever else abstract art may be, it is the most subjective of art expressions and, therefore, subject to the greatest variation in interpretation. Therein, perhaps, lies its chief interest as an art form.

PLATE 13

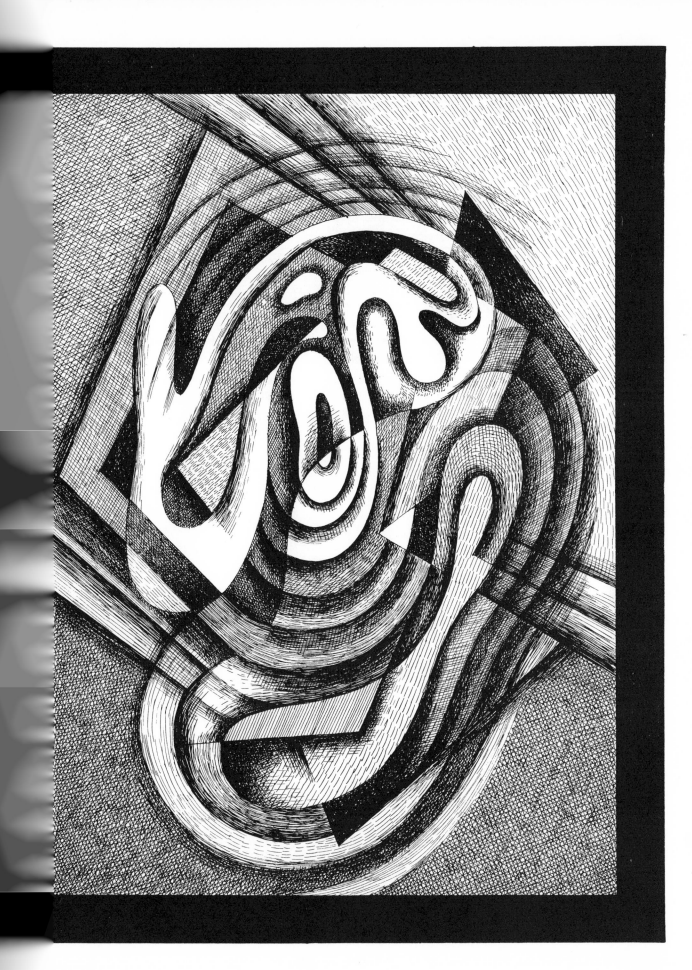

P L A T E 14. The plane surface.

IN FIGURE A: If line 3 moves through parallel positions, always touching two fixed parallel lines 1 and 2, a plane surface is generated.

IN FIGURE B: If through a fixed point (0), any number of straight lines is drawn intersecting a given straight line 1, then a plane surface is generated. (NOTE: Any randon straight line such as 2 may be drawn in a plane surface).

IN FIGURE C: A plane surface is shown in which are represented various types of plane figures. Sometimes the figure is identified by its contour (ellipse, triangle) and sometimes, as in the case of a line, it may be defined by its curvature. Whatever its name, as long as the figure lies wholly within the infinite plane surface, it is a plane figure.

IN FIGURE D: Intersection between two plane figures of unusual contour. Whatever the contour, the intersection is a straight line.

IN FIGURE E: When two parallel planes 2 and 3 are cut by a transverse plane 1, then the lines of intersection AB and CD are parallel.

IN FIGURE F: The intersection between three planes is a point (0).

IN FIGURE G: If non-parallel planes 1, 2, and 3 are cut by a transverse plane 4, the lines of intersection AB, CD, EF are not parallel.

The above statements represent some of the properties of plane surfaces.

A study of the properties of two and three-dimensional figures will yield fruitful results, especially for those who create in three dimensions (ceramists, metalry craftsmen, sculptors, architects, industrial designers, etc.).

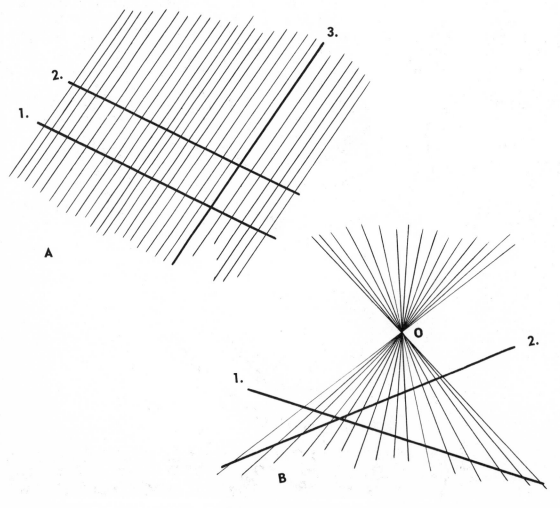

P L A T E 14

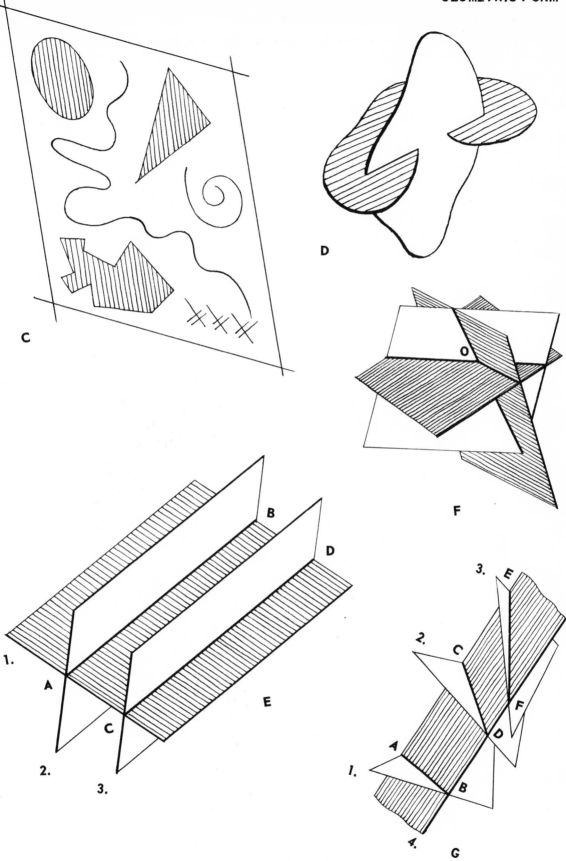

PLATE 15. Prismatic surfaces and solids.

If a straight line moves so that it remains parallel to a fixed straight line and always touches a succession of straight lines, a prismatic surface is generated. (The succession of straight lines may or may not form a closed space).

The total surface is composed of plane surfaces.

The prism may have any number of sides or faces, and each will be a plane surface.

If a prismatic surface is cut by any plane surface, the intersection will be a series of straight lines.

IN FIGURE 1: XY is the fixed straight line; CE is the moving line which always touches the lines AB, CD.

IN FIGURE 2: XY is the fixed straight line; DH is the moving line which always touches the lines AB, CD, EF.

IN FIGURE 3: XY is the fixed straight line; FG is the moving line which always touches the lines AB, CD, EF.

NOTE: Figure 3 illustrates an open prismatic surface while Figures 1 and 2 show closed prismatic surfaces.

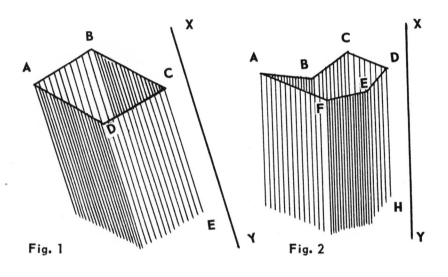

Fig. 1   Fig. 2

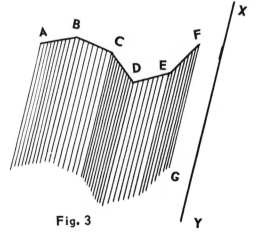

Fig. 3

PLATE 15

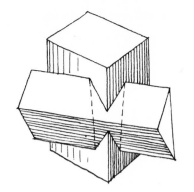

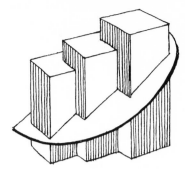

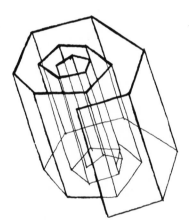

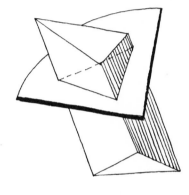

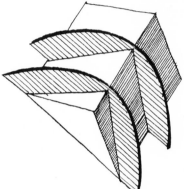

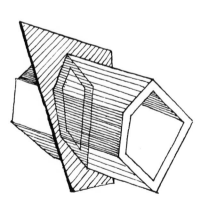

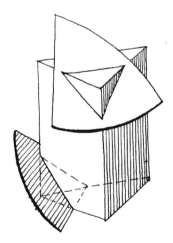

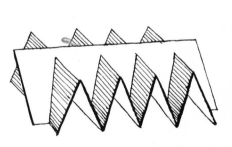

PLATE 15, continued

PLATE 16: If line 1 moves parallel to line A and always touches a fixed curve, a cylindric surface is generated.

If the curve is closed, the surface is a closed surface, as in Figure B.

If the curve is open, as in Figures C and D, the surface is an open surface.

The contour of a cylindric surface may be an irregular curve or a combination of curved and straight lines, as shown.

Remember that the character of any infinite surface is not altered by the line or lines which determine a small portion of the surface. (Illustrated in Figure C, Plate 14, this chapter).

The fixed line A and the fixed curve* are called directors of motion.

The moving line 1 is called the generator.

Theoretically, the generator is infinite in length and therefore the surface generated is an infinite surface.

* The fixed curve in Fig. B is M-M-M
The fixed curve in Fig. C is O-O-O
The fixed curve in Fig. D is P-P-P

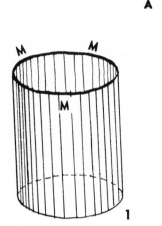

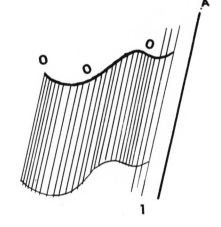

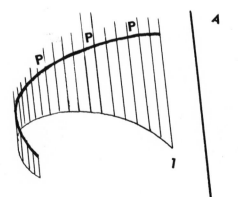

PLATE 16

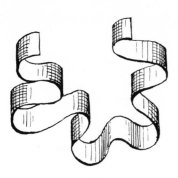
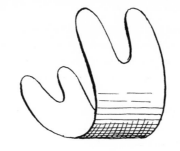
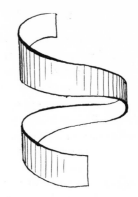

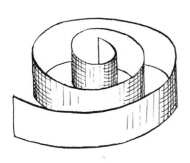
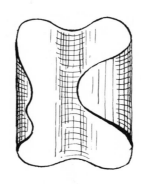
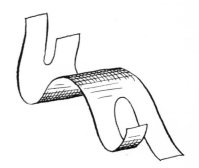

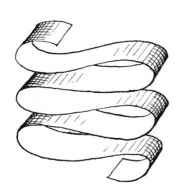
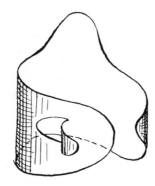
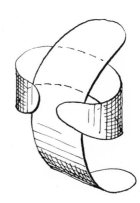

PLATE 16, continued

PLATE 17. Pyramidal surface.

If a moving straight line passes through a fixed point (0) and touches a succession of straight lines, open or closed, a pyramidal surface is generated.

The pyramid may have three or more lateral faces (Figures 1, 2, and 3).

Figure 4 is a frustum of a pyramid. The upper and lower bases are parallel to each other and are the same shape.

Figure 5 is a truncated pyramid in which the upper and lower bases are not parallel to each other and in general are neither the same shape nor size.

Figures 6 and 7 represent pyramidal surfaces.

Figures 8 and 9 show combinations of two pyramids. (Since all surfaces are plane surfaces, the lines of intersection must be straight lines).

Figure 10. Use of the pyramidal forms as simplification of complex natural forms. (Similar to transformation in plates on human, animal, and bird forms).

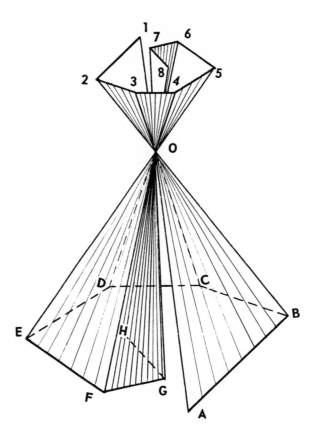

PLATE 17

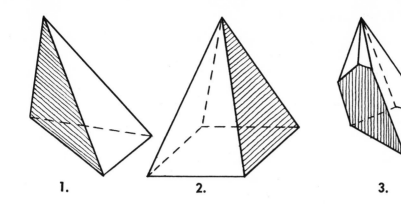

1.

2.

3.

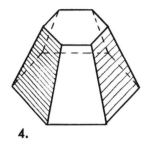

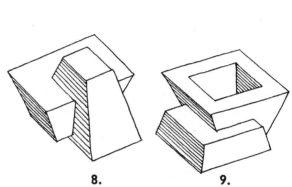

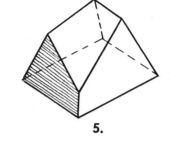

4.

5.

6.

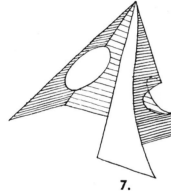

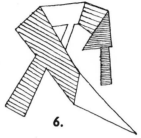

7.

8.

9.

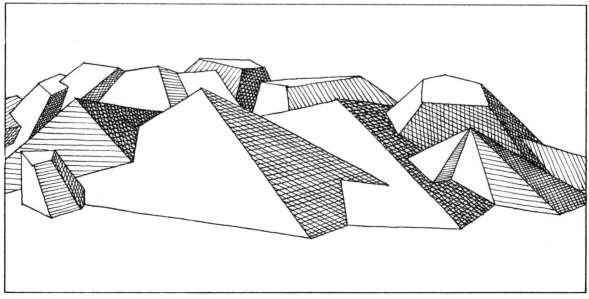

10.

PLATE 17 , *continued*

P L A T E 18 . Conical Surface.

If a straight line moves through a fixed point (O) and always touches a fixed curve, open or closed, a conical surface is generated.

Figures A to L represent conical surfaces. The straight lines represent elements of the surface, i.e., various positions of the generator.

The cylindric and conical surfaces can be unrolled into a plane surface. They are called developable surfaces. To put it another way, a plane surface can be transformed into a cylindric or conical surface without stretching and tearing.

Spherical, toroidal, and ellipsoidal surfaces cannot be converted into plane surfaces without deformation.

These facts are important to the designer because his design is often limited to a particular kind of surface due to manufacturing difficulties or limitations.

Figures 2, 3, and 4 show the intersection between planes and cones. In Figure 2, the plane is parallel to an element. The line of intersection is a parabola.

In Figure 3, the upper plane is parallel to the circular base. The line of intersection is a circle. The lower plane is oblique to the base. The line of intersection is an ellipse.

In Figure 4, the right plane passes through the apex cutting the base. The line of intersection is a triangle. The left plane makes an angle with the base that is greater than the angle that any element makes with the base. The line of intersection is a hyperbola.

The circle, ellipse, parabola, and hyperbola are called the conic sections.

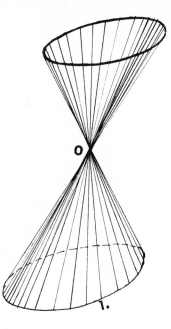

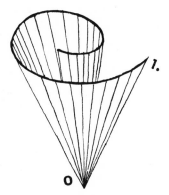

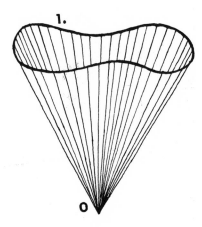

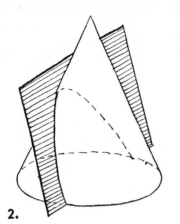

2.

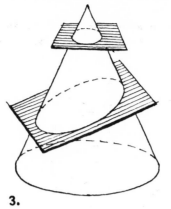

3.

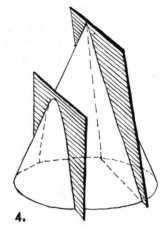

4.

A

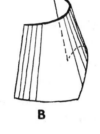

B

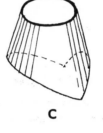

C

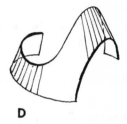

D

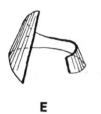

E

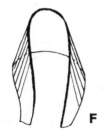

F

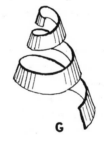

G

H

I

J

K

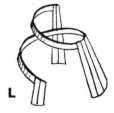

L

PLATE 18 , *continued*

PLATE 19. Rounded surface (surface of revolution). Egg-shaped or ellipsoid. Three-dimensional free form and variations.

The surface belongs to the general class of surfaces of revolution.

A surface of revolution is a surface generated by a line rotating about a straight line as an axis.

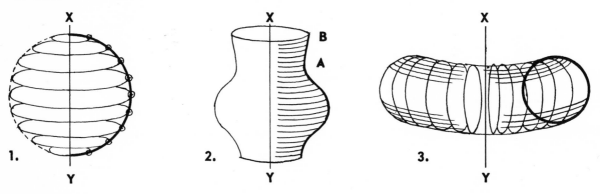

Each of the three figures shows how a surface of revolution is generated about a straight line, Axis X-Y.

IN FIGURE 1, a semi-circle moves, and each point on the semi-circle forms a complete circle as it moves through 360 degrees. The surface generated is spherical.

IN FIGURE 2, an irregular curve of which the upper part marked AB is a straight line rotates. The surface generated by the AB part is a conical surface, while the rest of the line generates a toroidal surface.

IN FIGURE 3, a circle rotates about the axis X-Y, generating a toroidal surface with a hole in the middle (somewhat similar to a doughnut). Successive positions of the moving circle are shown.

Surfaces of revolution are produced by spinning metal on a lathe.

A wood-turner generates surfaces of revolution by holding a cutting tool against a piece of wood as it rotates on an axis.

The ceramist working on a wheel originates surfaces of revolution. The axis of rotation is an imaginary line through the center of the wheel and at right angles to it.

The figures in Plate 19 show derivations of an egg-shaped solid. Figures 1, 2, 3, 4, 5, 6, 11, 12 are free forms.

Figures 7, 8, 9, and 10 are not free forms because each one of them has intersecting edges. The points in which the edges meet arrest the movement of the eye.

PLATE 19

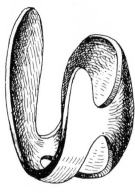

1.

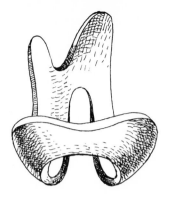

2.

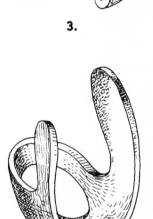

3.

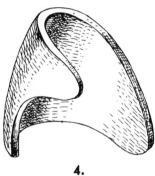

4.

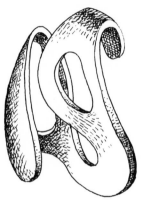

5.

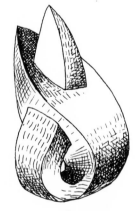

6.

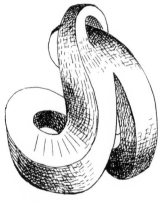

7.

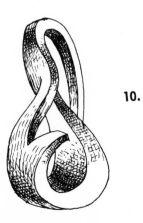

8.

9.

10.

11.

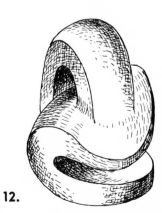

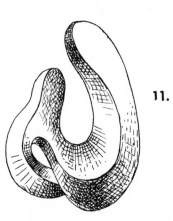

12.

SECTION TWO

FLOWER AND PLANT FORM

INTRODUCTION

I have made it a practice to do two things when I go to nature for my material. I draw with the greatest fidelity at my command the things that I have selected. Nothing is left out. If I am working in black and white, I jot down color notes. In effect, I try to draw the selected material without shifting or omitting anything. I call this the fact-finding stage. I have found this the best way of collecting authentic information. Then, using the same source material, I draw again, but this time I try to simplify the things I see by using simple basic geometric figures to express the complex natural objects. This gives me two separate and distinct types of information. (I call this the simplifying stage). The elements of design and composition do not enter stages 1 and 2. I do the actual designing after I have had a chance to study the material I got from nature. Sometimes, I return to the original setting and compose on the spot, but this is done only after the preliminary work has been accomplished.

There are many artists and designers who never compose from nature. They find it too confusing because of the many distractions. On the other hand, some insist that composing on the spot is the only way to work. My feeling about it is that each individual must work out the method that will best suit him. Whatever his decision, part of the procedure must include the collection of facts by direct observation.

Reference books and photographs should not be used by the beginner. It takes a lot of experience to use secondary material of this kind properly. Too often, the outside reference becomes a substitute for direct observation, and the prospective creator becomes an imitator. There is no way of knowing the precise time when any one person is ready to use second-hand material for his work. Each of us must be his own judge. The longer it is delayed, provided we get our information first-hand, the better.

The more we know about the way in which plants grow, their structure, shape , color, and environment, the greater the number of tools we have at our disposal for self-expression. The mere collection of facts, however, will not make artists of us. If we are clear about our aims, we need not worry on that score.

PLATE   1.   Let us start with the daisy. (Any flower that is more or less similar in structure will do).

FIGURE 1 in horizontal row A shows the flower as seen from above. Take a good look at Figure 1 and you will see:

(1) A center, whose shape is a small circle.

(2) Petals coming from the center (consider petals same in size and shape).

(3) The outer boundary or contour is circular.

(4) The individual shape of the petal and how the shape is repeated.

(5) Single lines and combinations of lines which represent part of a petal or part of a group of two or more petals (shown in row A by small line drawings).

(6) All lines either going toward or coming from the center (this is called a radial design).

The observations above are illustrated in horizontal row A and represent the first step in the actual creation of designs shown in vertical rows B and D.

What we have done so far is to examine the source material very carefully and to subdivide it into many different parts keeping in mind two very important features: first, the radial character, and next, the circular character of the flower.

Figure II in row A is composed of two circles and is called a simple geometric equivalent of the natural form.

Now we are ready to transform the natural object into a design by rearranging some or all the parts which appear in horizontal row A.

Look at the designs in vertical rows B and D. If you examine them you will see:

(1) Radial and circular arrangements (same as in the daisy).

(2) The motif is no longer the petal but a combination that has been put together from the material in horizontal row A.

(3) The established motif has been repeated (same as in the natural form).

(4) Some parts of the designs have been emphasized by making them darker. (By changing the light or dark emphasis, we can very effectively shift our interest from one part of the design to another).

(5) Vertical rows C and E show the motifs used to create the designs in row B. Numbers 2, 3, 4, in row C and numbers 5, 6, and 7 in row E show motifs to which repeat lines have been added. (Repeat lines are parallel lines whether straight or curved).

EXERCISE: Only eight motifs are shown in row A. Try to discover at least four more.

EXERCISE: Create a series of circular designs using combinations of motifs derived from the daisy. Make the motifs point toward the center.

EXERCISE: Using parts of the flower, add repeat lines to invent designs.

EXAMPLE:

EXERCISE: Select any one of the designs you create and study the effects created by a change in light and dark emphasis.

EXAMPLE:

Row A

B   C   D   E

PLATE 1

P L A T E   2.   The tulip provides the material for study in row A. Instead of looking into the flower as seen from above, a frontal position has been chosen.

We can divide the flower into two similar parts by a vertical line.   (Any straight line which divides a figure into two similar parts is called an axis of symmetry.)

In vertical row A:

The general shape of the outline or contour of Figure 1 is more or less triangular.

The inner part of the flower is composed of a central ellipse (M) and two triangular figures (N).

Not all the petals are the same shape and size.

The subdivisions or motifs show the effect of symmetry by the vertical axis.

N O T E :   Many more motifs can be derived from the flower as in Plate 1.

In vertical row B:

There are six variations in which the central part is the ellipse.   The ellipse remains the same in all the examples but the surrounding parts are changed.

Figure V shows the greatest change because there is no axis of symmetry.

In vertical row C:

All of the designs are asymmetric (no axis of symmetry).

In Examples II and VI two motifs are united by lines.   These lines are curved and are suggested by the curves in the flower itself and in the motifs taken from the flower, (Motifs M and N in row A).   Lines like these, used to unite two motifs or different parts of a design, serve as links or connections and are called transition lines.   (A straight line may also be used as a transition line.)

In Examples I, II, and III, only one half of the ellipse is used.

Example V is a rather free interpretation and seems to be less dependent on the source material than the other variations.   It has some of the character that you find in row B, a sort of second cousin relationship.   Basically, part of one motif was used, combined with transition lines. Can you discover the motif?

In vertical row D:

The daisy-type flower takes on a new look because of the direction from which we view it. A flower, or anything else for that matter, will very often show surprising differences in shape as we see it from different angles. (Only a perfectly round ball appears the same no matter how we look at it.)

(1) The general contour or outline is elliptical.

(2) It has an axis of symmetry. (Not strictly true but near enough for our purpose.)

(3) Each example emphasizes the symmetry.

(4) Each example shows how the petals are used in different ways.

E X E R C I S E S : 1. Create new combinations using the fundamental forms.

2. Use repeat lines on the outside as well as the inside forms.

3. Create asymmetric designs based on compositions in row D, using straight and curved lines separately and in combination.

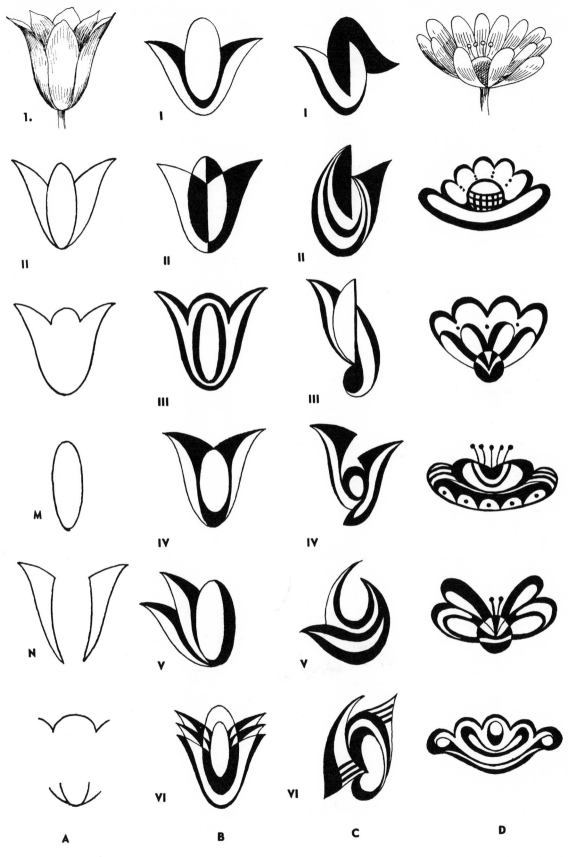

A

B

C

D

PLATE 2

P L A T E   3 .   If you haven't already suspected it, you will probably become aware of the importance of drawing as you go on with your creative work. Plate 3 stresses it because one of the most important ways of collecting material is to draw the things that interest you.

The drawings in Plate 3 represent a random collection of leaf, vegetable, fruit, and flower forms. They are part of my collection of sketches that I have made from nature and from models in the Museum of Natural History in New York City.

This group illustrates one of the ways in which material can be assembled. No attention is paid to composition. Draw the things that interest you in whatever order they appear. This represents step number 2. Step number 1 is the *desire and interest* to do it. What you do with the material is another problem, but before you can tackle it, you must have it *at hand*.

The names of the plants in Plate 3 are:

1. Pea pods and leaves;
2. Common caterpillar;
3. Moon fern;
4. Hawthorne;
5. Hawthorne;
6. Part of a cherry tree;
7. Gum plant;
8. Mustard leaves;
9. Poppy leaf.

E X E R C I S E :   Create a series of compositions in which combinations of plant forms are used.

E X A M P L E :

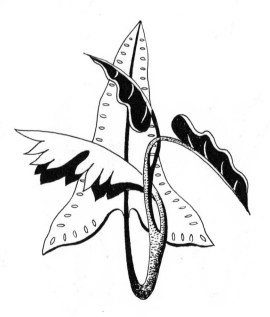

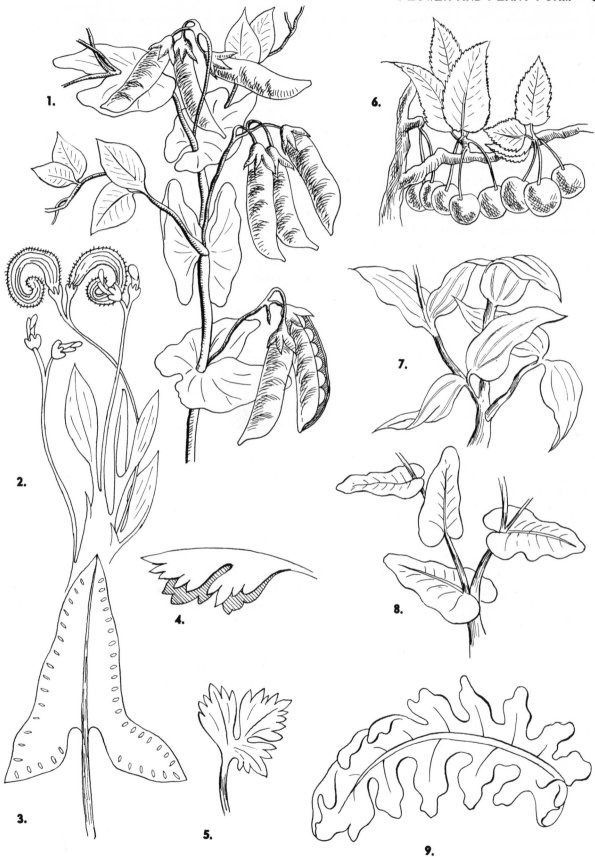

PLATE 3

P L A T E   4 .   The designs in this plate come from the source material of Plate 3. They represent only a very small fraction of the designs that are possible from such a wealth of material.

All the designs marked A and C are derived from the drawing of the leaves and pea pods marked 1 in Plate 3.

Before you inspect the A and C designs, turn back to Plate 3 and look carefully at drawing 1. Fix your mind on the general shapes of the different leaves as well as the pods. Notice the various curves formed by the veins in the leaves and by the stems.

Now turn to Plate 4 and you will see that the principal curves that give movement to the designs come from the curves in the natural form. This does not mean that they are an exact reproduction, but they are closely related. Sometimes only a very slight change from the object will give a most satisfactory result.

One good way to handle the problem of combining two or more leaves is to make an outline drawing of a leaf, cut it out of paper or cardboard, and then shift it about, drawing the outline for each new position. (The pattern is called a template).

The drawings marked C in Plate 4 make use of the peas, the pea pods, and the stems.

1.   Two of the designs feature the peas, while the third features the stem.

2.   Actually, the shape of the stem attachment and pea pod have not been changed very much. The changes from the natural form to the design form are due to:

a)   Making part of the natural form stand out more than it does in nature. (This is called emphasis).

b)   Repetition of same line. (This also creates emphasis).

N O T E :   All the designs in Plate 4 are asymmetric.

The designs marked B are derived from Figure 9 in Plate 3. It is a poppy leaf.

(1)   The irregular contour in the leaf itself is quite striking, and something of its character is retained in each variation.

(2)   The prominent central vein also plays an important role in the designs. It is a good idea to examine the source material, and any feature of it which impresses itself on you should be used.

(3)   Note how the small veins in the design differ from those in the leaf itself. (This is another example of emphasis.)

Figures A of Plate 4 represent combinations of two or more leaves found in drawings 1 and 7 of Plate 3.

Figures C are variations of peas and pea-pods found in Figure 1 of Plate 3.

Each arrangement is asymmetric. This follows, more or less, from the nature of the source material used, but there is no good reason why symmetric designs may not be created from this or any other material.

E X E R C I S E S :   Using Figures 2, 3, 4, 5, 6, and 8 of Plate 3 as source material,
(1) Create a series of closed designs.
(2) Combine Figures 4 and 5 to form a unit.

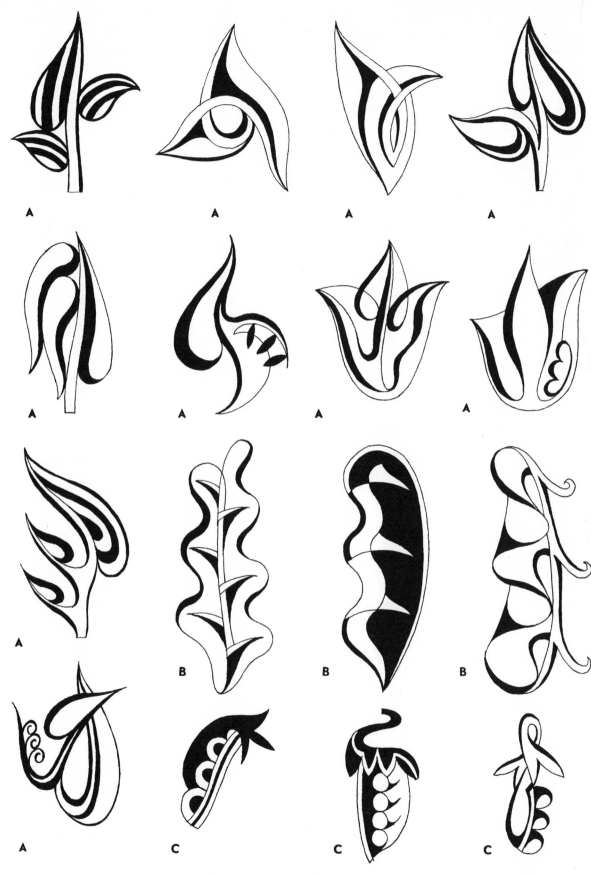

A A A A

A A A A

A B B B

A C C C

PLATE 4

P L A T E   5 . The composition shown in Plate 5 is made up of leaves, flowers, and ferns which grew alongside my house. The original pencil drawings made on the spot were, for the most part, separate drawings of the individual plants. Even though the general effect is one of realism and appears to be a faithful reproduction of the real thing, many liberties were taken with the actual forms and the order in which they grew alongside each other.

E X E R C I S E   1 : Use the plate as source material. Make separate drawings of the individual parts.

E X E R C I S E   2 : Using different combinations, unite the parts to invent compositions within rectangular spaces. (5 x 7 inches would be a good size for a beginning).

N O T E :   After you have made the separate drawings, close the book so that you will not be too much influenced by the original.

E X E R C I S E   3 : Figure 1 below shows the steps from realism in A to the skeletal arrangement in B to the abstract composition C. C makes liberal use of repeat lines.

Figure 1.
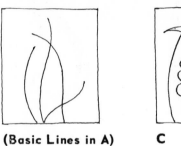

A   B   (Basic Lines in A)   C

A is an altered detail from Plate 5. To work out Exercise 3, use details from the compositions that you have created. Work out three steps as shown above.

PLATE 6. In this plate Figures A and B show combinations of leaves, while Figures C, D, and E illustrate compositions of flowers and leaves. The design of the flowers is based on the method used in Plate 1. The design of the leaves follows the method indicated in the five steps as illustrated below.

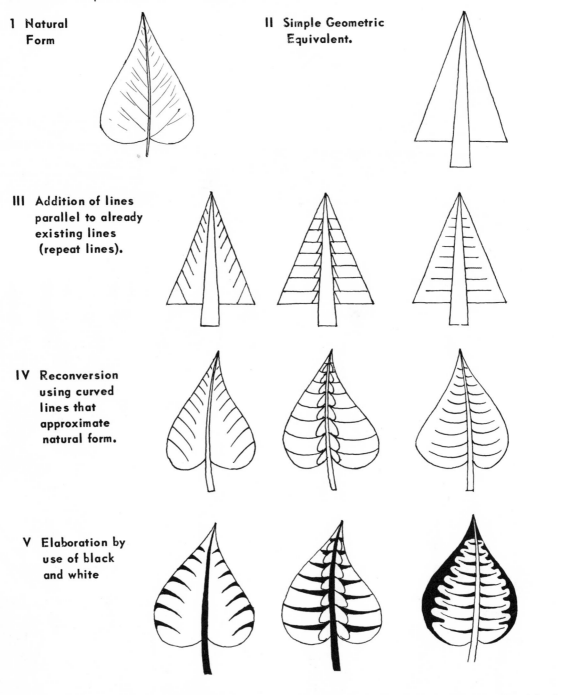

1 Natural Form

II Simple Geometric Equivalent.

III Addition of lines parallel to already existing lines (repeat lines).

IV Reconversion using curved lines that approximate natural form.

V Elaboration by use of black and white

EXERCISES: (1) Create a series of variations of Step III. Maintain control by keeping all auxiliary lines parallel to basic lines. Then convert by changing each straight line into a curved line.

(2) Combine leaves to form a composition within a square.

(3) Combine flowers to form a composition within a rectangle.

(4) Combine leaves and flowers to form a composition within a circle.

PLATE 6

P L A T E 7 . Cubic interpretation of fruits and vegetables.

Among natural objects, fruits and vegetables are relatively simple in shape. Because of their simplicity and also because they are readily available, they form a very useful group for study by painters, sculptors, and craftsmen.

If we leave out the element of color and confine ourselves to the problem of form, we can see that the two most common types are the cone-shaped, as the carrot, the pear, the beet; and the round-shaped, as the orange, the grapefruit, and the melon. Some, fewer in number, are a combination of both the round and the cone, as the turnip and the squash; while the banana, the acorn squash, and the pomegranate have a decidedly cubic feeling because of their well defined flat surfaces.

These descriptions in terms of figures in geometry are simplifications and do not tell the whole story about the shape of any one piece of fruit or vegetable, but they help us to fix in our minds the general shape. When we wish to make a drawing or a carving, or to fashion them in metal, we have a simple mental image to use as a guide.

The geometric figures become the simplest equivalents of the natural objects; just as in Plate 1 of this chapter, we saw how a circle under certain conditions might be considered the equivalent of the daisy.

The designer must develop the habit of reducing to the simplest possible shapes the complex things that he sees. When the habit becomes so much a part of him that he no longer has to think about it, he has probably reached a stage in his development at which he is quite adept at expressing himself.

Even the simplest objects in nature are quite complex, and the first job the designer has is that of doing something to make the difficult things easier to handle. This is when the process of simplification begins.

Suppose we start with a pear.

Natural Form:  Simplified Form:

These two drawings represent the complicated natural form and its simple interpretation. Between the two extremes we can have a great many forms, none of which will be as complex as the natural form nor as elementary as the simplified form.

The drawings in Plate 7 show in-between representations.

If you have ever tried to whittle a piece of wood into some kind of shape, or if you have ever carved in stone, or have used a flat piece of copper to raise an ash tray or bowl, or if you have ever tried to paint a still-life of fruit in a bowl, you will recognize the importance of the in-between figures. The connection between the drawings in Plate 7 and sculpture in wood, stone or metal is more obvious than the link with painting. Nevertheless, the painter is just as much concerned with problems of form as anyone else. In addition, the painter uses color which must heighten the effect of form.

As we increase the number of flat surfaces, the object as a whole takes on a rounder appearance. This means that we can make an object seem as round as we wish it to be by the the number of surfaces we decide upon. This fact is of special importance to the colorist because each flat surface can be made different in color from the adjacent ones, thereby creating interesting variations in color.

If you look at some of the paintings by Cezanne, Picasso, and Braque, you will see how they introduced flat surfaces in the rounded forms.

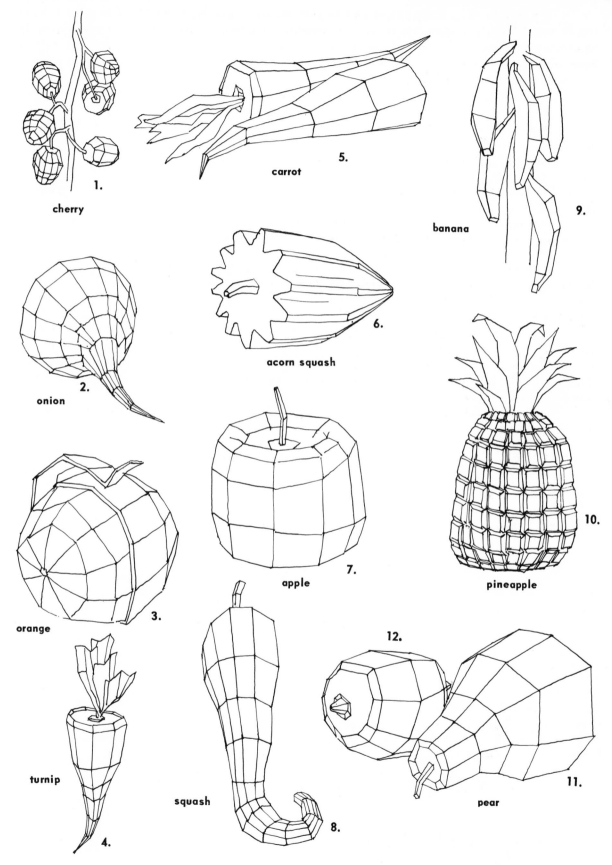

1.
cherry

5.
carrot

9.
banana

2.
onion

6.
acorn squash

3.
orange

7.
apple

10.
pineapple

4.
turnip

squash
8.

12.

11.
pear

PLATE 7

P L A T E   8 .   Everyone of us has seen trees. If you have ever tried to make a drawing of one of them, you know that it isn't the easiest thing to do. The tree is a complex form. It is composed of many different kinds of shapes that are the trunk, the branches, and leaf clusters. Some of the branches seem to come toward you, others to recede, giving the effect of huge masses that have a great deal of depth.

To handle source material of this kind, you must learn how to simplify the forms in nature. The drawings in Plate 8 suggest a way of doing this.

Method A.   Show only a small portion of the tree and leaves. (See Figures 5, 6, 9, 10, and 11).

Method B.   Do the tree as a whole, but make the trunk most important. (See Figures 1 and 2).

Method C.   Do the tree as a whole, but make the leaves most important. (See Figures 3, 4, 7, and 8).

Method D.   Change the various parts of the tree by using the simplest possible solids, (cylinders, cones, prisms, etc.) that will most nearly resemble the natural form.

Method A does not call for too much change from the natural form. It means concentrating the interest on one small part which you think will serve your purpose. Very little exaggeration or distortion is needed except for the purpose of emphasizing part of the design to give it added interest.

If you look at Figure 6 you will see what is meant. The left and right ends show the leaves with the curved branches similar enough to give both ends almost the same character. The two ends, important though they are, tend to balance each other somewhat like weights on a scale. This leaves the middle part free to receive the greatest attention. It becomes the center of interest or the area of chief interest.

Methods B and C call for considerable change from the original form. The distortion due to change in size of one part begins the process of abstraction.

EXERCISE: Leaf clusters, two and three-dimensional shapes.

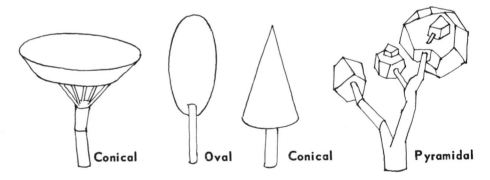

Conical   Oval   Conical   Pyramidal

EXERCISE: Combine trees drawn in simplified form to create compositions.   **EXAMPLES:**

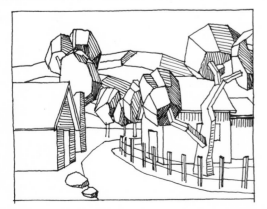

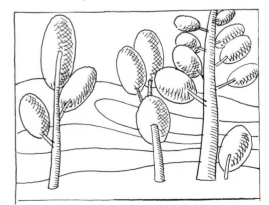

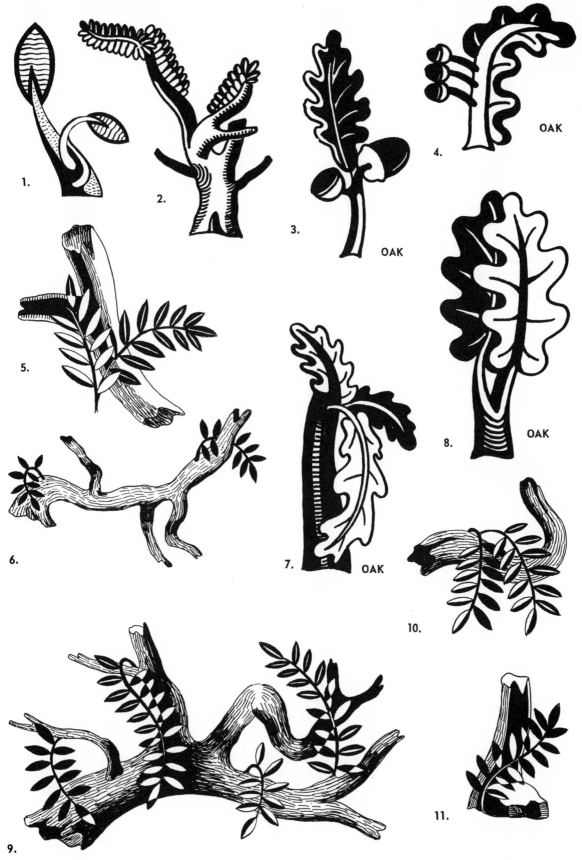

1.

2.

3.   OAK

4.   OAK

5.

6.

7.   OAK

8.   OAK

9.

10.

11.

PLATE 8

P L A T E   9 .   This plate represents a number of designs based on combinations of leaves and flowers, leaves and vegetables.

Do you recall Plate 6 of this chapter? It also has some designs based on leaf and flower combinations. As in Plate 6, stress is laid on putting down a few lines that will show you how the various parts of the design will fit.

Let us take Figure 5 of Plate 9 as an example. The basic linear plan is shown in Figure A.

Fig. A.

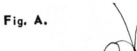

There are five different elements that compose the ensemble, and they can be put together in many different ways. Some of the new arrangements may be better or worse than the one shown, but unless we try some of them, we shall never know.

These are the new combinations:

F I G U R E 7 is derived from the pea and pea-pod in Plate 3.

F I G U R E 8 is derived from the cherry in Plate 3.

F I G U R E 1 is based on an acorn and a common variety of leaf that is not an oak leaf. (Botanists may object to the combination).

F I G U R E 2 is based on the artichoke.

F I G U R E 3 is based on the squash.

F I G U R E S 4, 6 and 11 are leaf and flower groups that are not based on any one particular species, but are inventions, using parts of different flowers.

F I G U R E 5 is based on the tiger lily.

F I G U R E S 9 and 10 are based on an ear of corn.

F I G U R E 12 is based on the top of a pineapple.

You must decide how imitative your design will be. This is a personal matter in which you are the sole judge. If you are commissioned to do something and must follow someone else's ideas, you are actually sharing most of the problems with him. There are times when this may prove to be a handicap, but the designer who uses his imagination and resourcefulness will generally overcome the difficulties that arise from such collaboration.

Figures 7, 8, 11, and 12 show the greatest divergence from the natural form.

E X E R C I S E :   Use the source material in Plates 3 and 5 to design combinations of plants.

1.

2.

3.

4.

5.

6.

7.

8.

9.

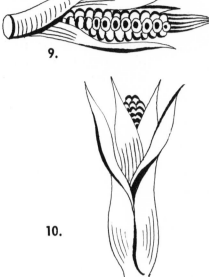

10.

11.

12.

PLATE 9

P L A T E 1 0 .   This plate shows a group of compositions within rectangles based on plant form. In each example, the flower or leaf form is the center of interest. The subordinate parts are combinations of straight or curved lines that are used to add interest to the designs as a whole and at the same time help emphasize the plant figures.

Examine each composition for the following:

(A) Variety in the shapes of spaces produced by the lines.

(B) Different emphasis produced by distribution of lights and darks.

(C) Basic linear scheme.

(D) Feeling of movement created by the flow of line.

(E) The way in which balance between various parts is maintained.

(F)   The types of line and space used to create a feeling of unity. (Unity means that all the parts of a design fit together, and if one part is taken out or altered, the design, as a whole, suffers).

(G) Is the center of interest or the area of chief interest clearly defined? (Study each example and compare).

E X E R C I S E :   Start with a rectangular frame and create basic layouts for compositions based on plant form.

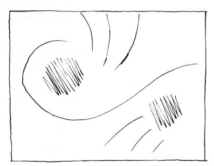

Stage I of layout

Stage II of layout

Stage I shows the barest outline.

Stage II is more complete. The various parts are elaborated.

Stage III is the addition of lights and darks (or color).

Stage IV is the final stage in which refinements are added. (Very often stage III may be the the final one).

N O T E :   Use your own motif material for these problems.

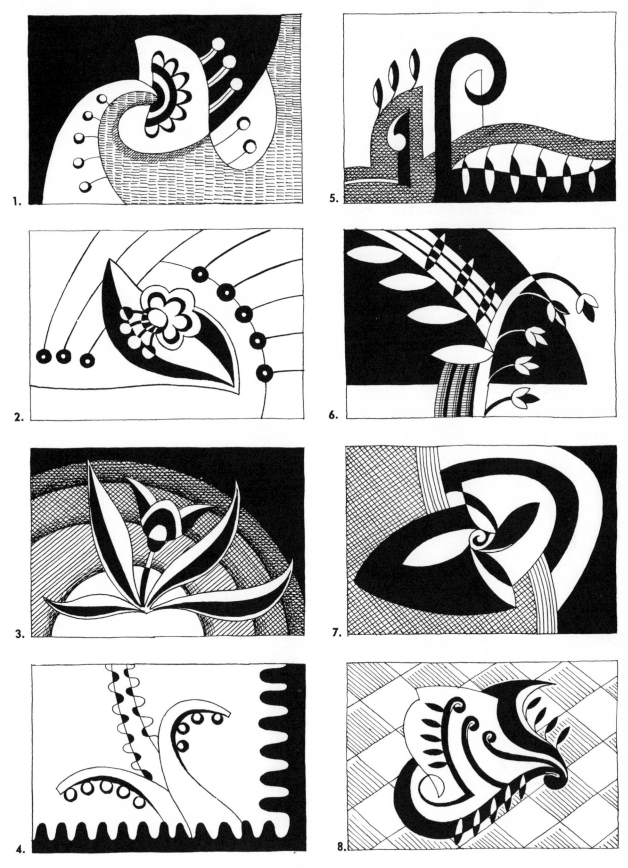

1.

2.

3.

4.

5.

6.

7.

8.

PLATE 10

P L A T E   11.   With the exception of Figure 4, outdoor settings have been used as the basis for the arrangements combining plant and man-made forms. In Figures 2 and 6, the man-made parts play a minor role, whereas in Figures 1, 3, and 5, the man-made part, which in each case is a house, is almost as important as the plant form. It is not good practice to give equal importance to two or more diverse elements of your design because each of the equally important parts will claim your attention at the same time, and the result will be confusion.

Make up your mind in advance which type of source material you wish to feature and as you proceed, stop to examine what you are doing, and ask yourself whether you are retaining or losing control of the basic idea with which you started.

The compositions in Plate 11 may be grouped as follows:

Figure 1 is partially radial.

Figures 2, 6, and 4 are essentially radial.

Figures 3 and 5 are essentially triangular.

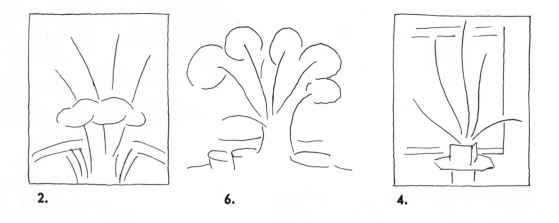

2.   6.   4.

3.   1.   5.

N O T E :   In each example a naturalistic setting has been used. In spite of consider-able simplification of form, the general effect is not too far removed from reality.

1.

2.

3.

4.

5.

6.

PLATE 11

PLATE 12.   In this plate combinations of plant and human forms have been used. The human form has been made secondary in importance. In Figures 1 and 6, the human forms play only a negligible role in design , whereas in Example 4, the climbing figure is much more important. This illustrates the importance of control, and we, as the designers, must decide in advance how much emphasis we shall give to the various parts of our arrangement, and we must stick to it. This does not mean that we may not at times change our ideas as to the relative importance of the parts, but if we do not discipline ourselves to think things out first, we shall find that we keep changing our designs constantly. I know from personal experience how important it is to take the time and make the effort to arrive at some clearly defined idea. It is just as important to carry through with this idea. After the idea is down on paper, changes can be made if necessary. Incidentally, there are very few designs, simple or complex, that do not undergo some change from the original mental concept.

Note in each example how the human figure has been modified to conform to the general character expressed in the plant forms.

NOTE: A line surrounding each of the designs forms a comparatively simple closed space. Figure 2 shows the contour to be a modified triangle.

EXERCISE: Create a series of arrangements combining plant and human forms in which the plant form is dominant:
(1) The chief characteristic of the design is the angularity. Example (a).
(2) The chief characteristic of the design is the flowing, curved lines. Example (b).
(3) The chief characteristic of the design is the use of straight and curved lines. Example (c).

Use different contours.

(a)

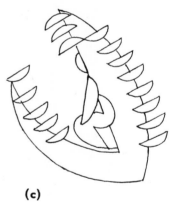

(b)   (c)

1.

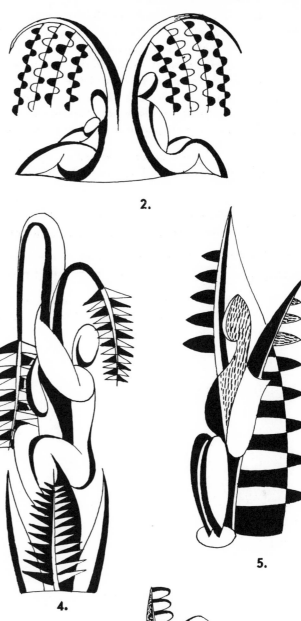

2.

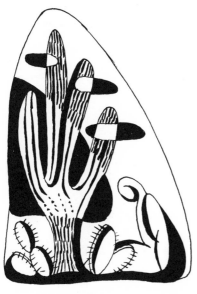

3.

4.

5.

6.

7.

PLATE 12

PLATE 13. In Plate 13, the same type of animal was used in each of the arrangements. The angular modifications in Figures 1 and 9 were dictated by the need for conformity with the character of the plant design.

With the exception of Figure 9, the flower and plant parts of each design are the dominant ones. In Figure 9, the plant portion of the design is a little more important than the animal, but there is no dominance. The lack of dominance creates tension, because the two differing motifs of almost equal importance claim our attention at the same time. In general, avoid using motifs of equal or almost equal importance in a single composition.

NOTE: This generalization, as almost all others, particularly in art, is subject to many exceptions. It is a good working rule, however, for those with little or no experience.

NOTE: When a design is symmetrical, each part of the arrangement about the axis of symmetry is of equal importance. (See Plate 2, row D in this chapter). In this case the dominant area will be along the axis of symmetry, generally the least important part of the design.

NOTE: Symmetry is almost never used in pictorial design. (I have never seen a perfectly symmetrical easel painting or mural. I doubt that there is one).

In Plate 13, Figures 1, 5, and 6 are based on modified symmetry. Figure 3 is radial. Figures 4, 5, and 8 are modified radial. Figure 9 is based on opposition of dominant areas. (See Plate 4 in the chapter on composition).

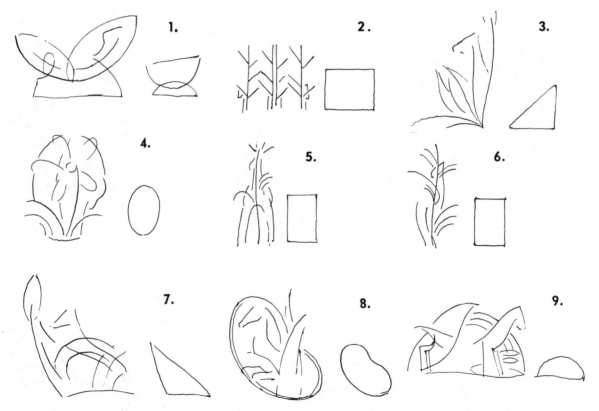

Basic contours in Figures 2, 5, and 6 are rectangular; in Figures 3 and 7, triangular; in Figures 4 and 8, elliptical; and in Figures 1 and 9, semi-circular.

PLATE 13

P L A T E 14 .   In this plate reptilia have been combined with flower and plant forms. (Exception Figure 3).

The methods used in Plates 11, 12, and 13 have been followed here.

The normal contours of the realistic forms have not been changed beyond recognition .

Analyze the eight designs for:

    (1)   Various ways in which leaves and plants have been drawn.

    (2)   Relationship of flow of line between plant and reptile.

    (3)   Outline and its approximation of relatively simple geometric shape.

    (4)   Area of chief interest.

Illustrations of Analysis:

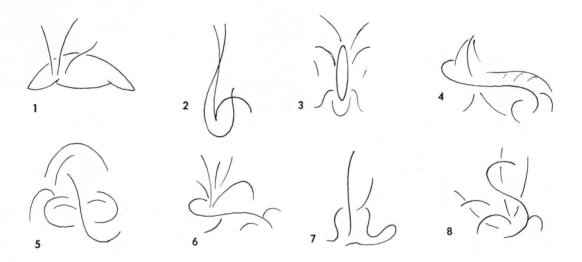

E X E R C I S E :   Rearrange basic lines of illustrations above and complete designs by adding necessary details.

E X A M P L E :

PLATE 14

PLATE 15.   The **one**   part of Plate 15 consists of six interpretations of the dragon tree based on variations of the trunk and leaf clusters. Even though the designs seem far removed from the original, the actual changes are not radical.

Greater variety can be achieved by reducing the repetition of the same clusters.

First, when using a tree as source material, try to get an over-all picture of the extreme contours of the tree as a whole and of several of the leaf clusters.   Then reduce these contours to the simplest geometric forms.

Observe carefully the character of the trunk and main branches.   The way in which the trunk divides or the way in which the branches twist and turn will suggest patterns and rhythms that will be very useful.   The statements above apply equally to a consideration of the volume or three-dimensional nature of the tree.   Just as there are simple plane equivalents, there are simple mass or volume equivalents of natural forms.

The other part of Plate 15 shows a group of variations of tree forms in which comparative-ly simple solids have been used to express and interpret the complex natural forms.

For the most part pyramidal and cylindrical forms have been used.

N O T E :   Consult the chapter on geometric form.

PLATE 15

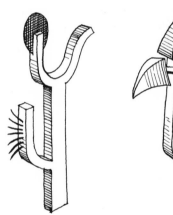

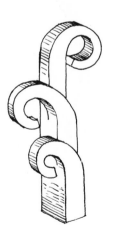
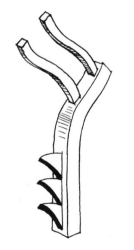
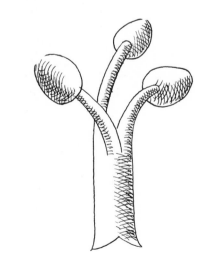

PLATE 15, continued

PLATE 16.   This plate deals with a series of three-dimensional interpretations of tree forms.

The natural forms of trunks and limbs of trees may be divided into two groups, cylindrical and conical.   The leaf clusters may assume a great variety of shapes, the most common being ellipsoidal, spherical, partially conical, and cylindrical, and combinations of those mentioned.

Careful observation will be very rewarding because it will enable the designer to introduce order and control into something that seems at times to be beyond control.

NOTE: Study the three-dimensional figures in the chapter on geometric form.

In Plate 16, Figure 1 is an interpretation of a tree trunk in which plane surfaces are used for all the parts. This is sometimes called a cubic equivalent. All rounded objects lend themselves to this type of expression.   The use of it is strongly recommended because in many respects it is the easiest to comprehend and to use.

NOTE: In each chapter at least one plate deals with and illustrates the cubic equivalent of natural form.

The character of the design that you create will be very strongly influenced by the medium in which you work and the skill with which you use your tools.

If you evolve a design which offers difficulties of execution beyond your present capacity, modify the design to fit your talents.

This is a common problem, and all designers, beginners and experts alike, are confronted with it.   Don't let it scare you.

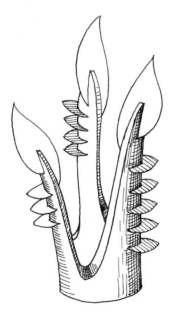
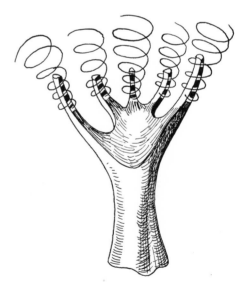

PLATE 16

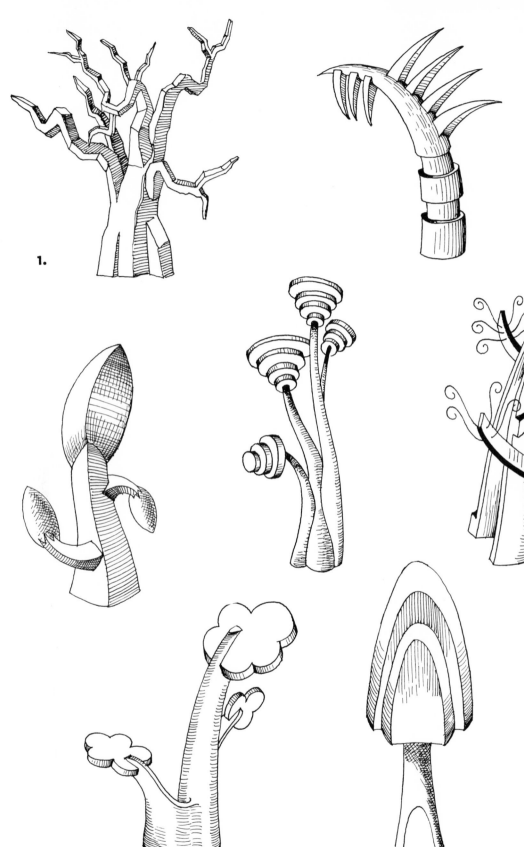

1.

PLATE 16 , continued

SECTION THREE

BIRD AND ANIMAL FORM

INTRODUCTION

Birds and animals are restless creatures. This is almost always true when you try to draw them from life. They never seem to stand still. Despite this difficulty, from the cave men of Spain and France to the present day, animals have played a very important role as subject matter in design.

The men who scratched the outlines of animals in dimly lit caves, those who carved them in relief on buildings, the ceramists who painted them on clay must have spent a great deal of time observing them. There were no reference books, no cameras, and for thousands of years there was no paper on which sketching could be done. Handicaps that seem frightening to us today did not deter the artists and designers of times past.

Two things are of the greatest importance in drawing; first, training the memory, and second, learning how to omit non-essentials.

Let us consider the memory aspect of drawing. To begin with, drawing is a process by which we first observe something, and then with pencil or charcoal, we record some of the things that we remember about the object. When our pencil is touching the paper, we do not look at the object. We are occupied with the graphic rendition of the thing as we remember it. Drawing becomes a constant, almost rhythmic change from observation to rendition and back to observation. It is true that the intervals during which our eyes are not on the object are of short duration, but however short, during that period we must remember, or we have nothing to put down.

The good draughtsman has developed the faculty for remembering the things that he is interested in and he has also developed through long experience the ability to retain salient facts about the remembered things. He has attained this highly desirable faculty only through constant practice.

The good drawing is often distinguished for the things that it leaves out, rather than for the things that it includes. This brings us to the second consideration: what can we omit and still give adequate expression to the things we wish to say?

Drawing begins with observation. We observe the action of the figure; how it retains its equilibrium, what the general contours are, the relative proportions of the essential parts, the direction of critical lines, and a host of other things. The greater our experience, the more we see and the more we retain.

The designer doesn't function merely as an agent who itemizes and catalogues each and every feature as if he were making an inventory for someone's inspection. He wants to invest his work with power and life and give it meaning that goes far beyond anything that mere imitation can accomplish. To make his meaning more decisive, he creates his own emphasis, pointing up some features at the expense of others, and omitting some altogether. He must know what he wants to say. He must be definite in his own mind before he can put down anything with effectiveness. The omissions are the result of all the study, experiments, observations that must precede any serious attempt at self-expression.

There is a great deal more to drawing than memory and selection. We need to know something about the anatomical structure of the figure if we hope to express ourselves adequately.

I think that comparative anatomy is important to the designer. The human figure is taken as the basic figure. Then anatomy of birds and animals can be profitably studied in relation to human anatomy. As an example, the wings of a bird correspond to the arms of a man. If we study the similarities and differences, we shall find that it is not too difficult to draw the bird in flight, showing various positions of the wings as the bird does different things. This is just one instance of how we can study and learn about the forms we have to deal with by relating them to other objects. This method is decidedly useful, not only when the anatomy of the figures is being considered, but it is very helpful when we compare the three-dimensional aspects of

the various major subdivisions of the figures. As an example, compare the head of a bird, excluding the beak, with the head of a horse or cow. We might say that the head of a bird is essentially spherical, that of a horse, pyramidal. If we make these comparisons, we not only develop definite mental images of each part of the individual figures, but we can more easily assemble the parts to create a whole. More than this, as we become better acquainted with one group, we learn more about other types because we have built up an awareness of the relationships that exist.

The more we know, the easier it is for us to exploit our knowledge and make it work for us. We can be literal, we can be fancy-free, or we can be both at the same time.

PLATE 1. The drawings in this plate are somewhat similar to the skeletal draw-ings in Plate 1 of the human figure. There is a marked similarity between the two that is not apparent at first sight.

Figure 1

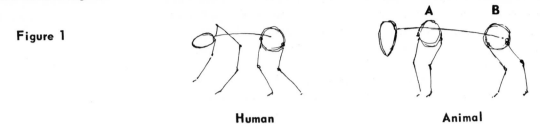

Human   Animal

The action of the arms and hands in the human correspond to the action of the hind legs of the animal (Figure 1.). The action of the legs and feet in the human correspond to the front legs of the animal. (In the elephant, the motion of the front and hind legs is the same corres-ponding to the legs of a human being.)

A knowledge of these facts gives you a working basis for the simplified structure of the animal figure.

The distance between the shoulder region (A) and the pelvic region (B), in Figure 2 be-low, depends upon the amount of foreshortening desired.

Figure 2

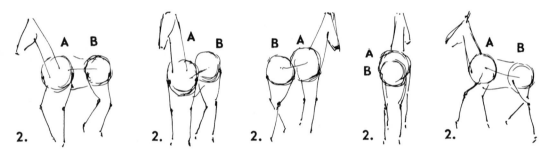

Exaggeration, shortening, and omission of parts of the figure play an important part in creating animal design:

1. Elongation of neck, body, or feet.
2. Shortening of neck, body, or feet.
3. Omission of thickness of various parts of the figure.

The use of any one of the above is a good starting point in the transformation of the realistic form into a design form.

A design is an arrangement in which one or more features of the natural object has been omitted or changed. As more changes are made, the design retains fewer recognizable features. The design is now more abstract than it was in the first instance. A pure abstract design is one in which all relationships and identification with natural and man-made objects have been com-pletely eliminated.

Whether or not the attainment of the goal, pure abstraction, can ever be achieved in art is a question which need not concern us in this book.

EXERCISE: Make series of skeletal drawings of animals, showing variety of action.

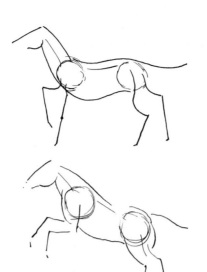
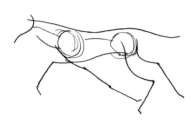
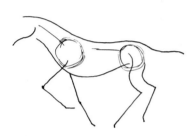
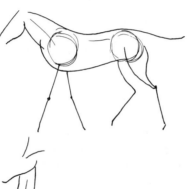
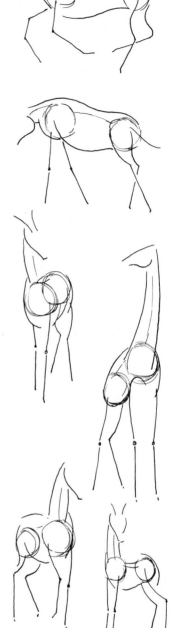

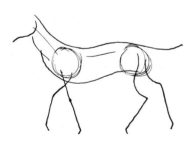

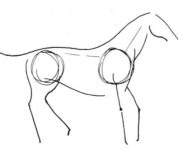

PLATE 1

PLATE 2.   Consider Figure B of Plate 2.

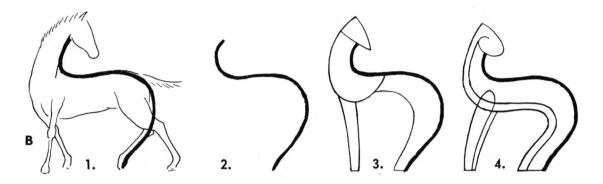

Figure 2. The heavy line in Figure 1 has been removed and forms the central idea from which will come a new arrangement. Many new combinations are possible, such as Figures 3, 4, and 5.

Even in a drawing such as Figure B, which is hardly more than an outline, it is possible to find many lines not necessarily curved which are an intrinsic part of the figure, both for contour and action, and which can be used as shown.

EXERCISES:
(1) Make drawings from actual animals.
(2) Go to a museum of natural history, if it is conveniently located.
(3) Work from photographs (only as a last resort).

I have tried to stress the importance of going directly to the source material. There is no better way. Drawing from the actual object, difficult though it may sometimes be, helps you to train your power of observation and memory and gives you first-hand experiences which form a reservoir, from which you can draw many times, to help your design.

I do not say 'Do not use photographs'. I do say, 'Use them very sparingly and certainly not until you have gone a long way with your design'. The beginner should under no circumstances use photographs, nor should photographs of unfamiliar objects be used.

My only justification for suggesting that you use some of my source material is that I want you to work out the methods in design. Until you gather your own original material, your design will not be original.

EXERCISE: Do a series of designs based on fundamental lines as shown above.

The drawings marked A, B, C, D, E are very simple sketches of a horse. The designs which have been created from the sketches show how variations from the natural form will give character to a design.

Variety can be achieved by:
(1) Changing emphasis from one part of a figure to another (Figures K, P)
(2) Changing flow of line (Figures G, M)
(3) Changing relative proportions of figures (Figures F, L)
(4) Changing the shapes of the major parts (Figures H, N)

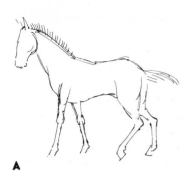

A

F

L

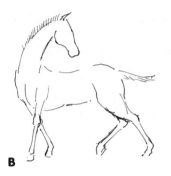

B

G

M

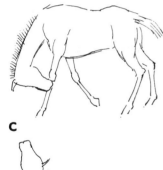

C

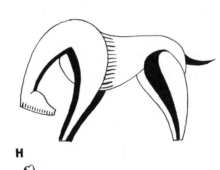

H

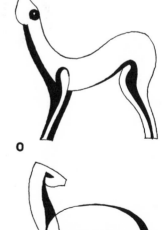

N

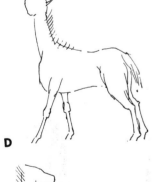

D

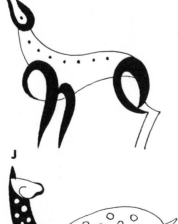

J

O

E

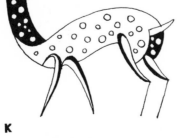

K

P

PLATE 2

P L A T E   3.   In this plate vertical row A shows an animal whose torso and legs remain fixed while the positions of the head and neck have been changed.

If you examine the five sketches, you will see that a change of position of one or more parts will affect the shape of the figure as a whole. The change in shape and consequent change in movement provide the designer with new material for invention.

In general, when an object is composed of several major parts that control shape and movement, whether human, animal, or bird, begin with a simple position of the figure. Sketch variations by changing the action of one of the major parts. Before you change the positions of two or more parts, complete the variations relating to a change of position of one part.

The major divisions of an animal are: 1. head, 2. neck, 3. torso (body), 4. front legs, 5. hind legs, 6. tail.

Each one of the divisions gives rise to quite a few positions independent of the other parts.

If you increase the possible changes in action by combining two or more parts, the number of different positions will run into astronomical figures. You need never worry about exhausting all the possibilities.

There may not be a great difference between some of the variations, but as you become more sensitive to form and movement, even the slight changes will stimulate a flow of new ideas.

E X E R C I S E S : Start with any basic position of the animal.
(1) In simple outline, draw variations of the basic position.
(2) Your design does not have to show every part of the animal.
(3) Take advantage of the rhythms in the source material.
(4) Use all curved lines.
(5) Use all straight lines.
(6) Use combinations of straight and curved lines.
Study the examples in Plate 3 for illustrations of the suggestions listed above.

A

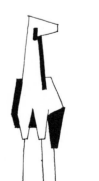

P L A T E   3

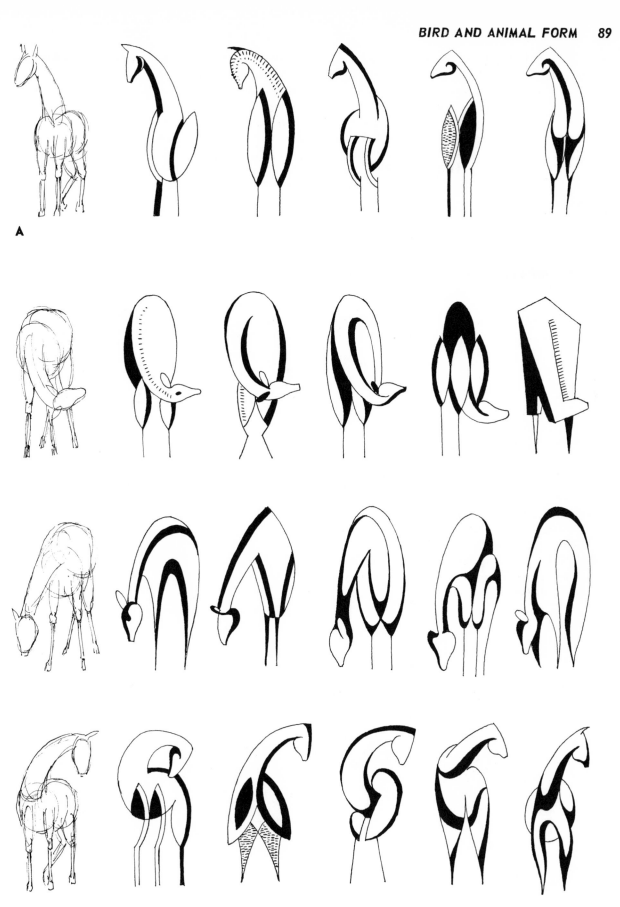

A

PLATE 3, *continued*

P L A T E   4 .   This plate illustrates how motifs can be repeated to create added interest.

(1) Parallel positions (asymmetrical) Figures F, J, and T.

In Figures F and T, the figures move along a horizontal line.

In Figure J, the figure moves along a sloping line.

(2) Bilateral symmetry — All the figures except F, G, H, J, P, and T.

(3) Upside-down position — Figures G, H, and P.

(Figure H forms part of a circular design.)

E X E R C I S E S :   1. Use some of the animal figures you have invented. Use the three different types of repetition to get combinations.

2. Change the distribution of light and dark areas to place chief interest in different parts of the arrangements.

E X A M P L E :

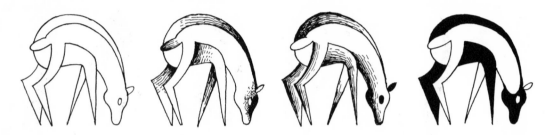

Study the surface markings of the natural forms for possible use in creating different decorative treatments.

When the shape of a figure is such that it can be divided into two similar parts by a straight line, the line is called an axis of symmetry, and   the figure has bilateral symmetry.

N O T E : Some figures have more than one axis of symmetry. When a figure has no axis of symmetry, it is called asymmetric.

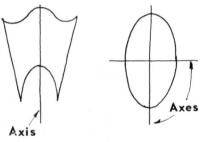

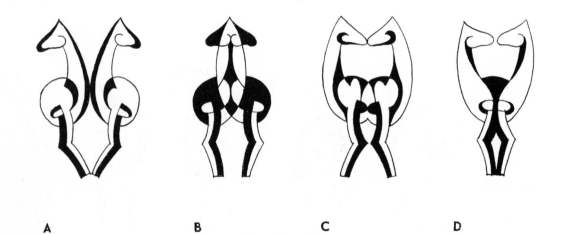

A   B   C   D

P L A T E   4

E

F

G

H

J

K

L

M

N

O

P

Q

R

S

T

U

PLATE 4 , continued

P L A T E   5 .   Cubic representation of the animal form is similar in treatment and approach to that of any other natural form, including the human.

Such treatment and study helps to build a vivid concept of three-dimensional form and makes it much easier to work with complex objects.

There is a considerable amount of historic precedent for this approach beginning with the Egyptians, going on to Archaic Greek Art, then through Albrecht Dürer, and many others.

Theoretically, a rounded surface is composed of an infinite number of plane surfaces. It is impossible to draw all of them. Therefore, a choice has to be made and we try to select those planes which will retain the general character of the form and give us, at the same time, the feeling of bulk-weight or mass.

A curved line may be considered as being composed of an infinite number of points, each point being the intersection of two straight lines.

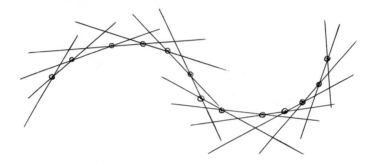

E X E R C I S E : Use figures in Plate 1 and your own figures. Make cubic drawings of them.

The animal form can be expressed by simplified three-dimensional magnitudes which have rounded surfaces, just as in the case of the human form.

The basic solid forms are the following: (See chapter on Geometric form.)

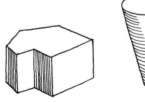

Prism   Cylinder   Cone   Pyramid

 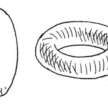 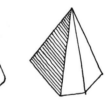

Sphere   Ellipsoid   Torus

E X E R C I S E : Make drawings and models, using combinations of basic solid forms.

PLATE 5

P L A T E   6 .   These are fundamental forms in which each of the major divisions of the bird has been simplified.

The major divisions are (1) head, (2) neck, (3) wings, (4) body, (5) tail, (6) legs.

When the neck is very short, as it is in many cases, it may be disregarded.

The lines which make up the fundamental form, in general, include contour lines, both extreme and inner, and action lines. The action lines suggest the movement of the bird.

The fundamental forms which in effect are simplified statements of the complex natural form may be drawn with straight and curved lines or solely with straight lines.

The fundamental form should be a simple form; how simple depends upon the source material and how much of it can be eliminated, while preserving a recognizable semblance of the original.

Because the natural form is always very complex, more than one simple interpretation is possible. This is a repetition of the statement made in connection with the use of the human form in design and bears repeating because we are apt to forget that all of our source material, with the exception of the geometric form, must be simplified before we can use it.

Design involves a change from the natural order. The natural order includes not only the positions and sizes of the parts in relation to each other in a single thing but also the positions and sizes of the whole forms with respect to one another.

The same position of an animal or a bird form, when seen from different angles, will result in entirely different contours and changes of relative proportions of the various parts. When drawing from the actual form, make as many sketches as possible of the same pose from different positions. This is important not only because it gives you more source material but also because the variety of views, when used for reference, gives a more comprehensive picture of the three-dimensional form.

PLATE 6

PLATE 6, continued

P L A T E   7 .   The source material is the pigeon. Rows B and C show a number of variations on the same theme. I have purposely confined myself to curved lines. Notice how in some of them the body is emphasized, in others, the wings, and several feature the head and neck.

In row A, source material is shown which is to be used as the basis for the following exercises:

EXERCISE 1:   Create a series of fundamental forms — A (all curved), B (all straight), C (straight and curved).
E X A M P L E , row A, Figure 3:

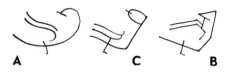

EXERCISE 2:   Create a series of designs elaborating the fundamental forms.
E X A M P L E , row A, Figure 3:

E X E R C I S E 3 :   Combine two or more to form complete units.

E X A M P L E : Combination of Figures 2 and 3 in row A.

E X A M P L E : Combination of Figures 4, 3, and 1, in row A.

1.

2.

3.

4.

5.

A   B   C

PLATE 7

PLATE 8.   The hooded merganser is the theme from which all of the variations were made. As in Plate 7, curved lines are used almost exclusively.

In most of the variations, the bodies and heads have been featured. This is due to the influence of the unusual headdress and the markings on the body.

In studying source material, the various aspects of the forms must be taken into account in order that you get the most out of the material.

(1) Study the following <u>two-dimensional aspects</u>:

A. Contours
B. Surface markings
C. Relative sizes of the parts
D. Action

E. General character of the figure as a whole.
   (Graceful, heavy, fleet, etc.)
F. Textural quality of the various parts
G. Color

(2) Study the following <u>three-dimensional aspects</u>:

A. General character of form as a whole
B. Three-dimensional forms of the major parts
C. The plane construction of the figures

An investigation into the properties listed makes for better acquaintance with the material and gives more tools with which to work.

The above list is by no means intended to be exhaustive, but it will serve as a working basis.

The list is intended for general use and includes all the categories of source material. Some forms, by their very nature, are two-dimensional and will have fewer properties to consider than others.

For instance, a leaf may be considered two-dimensional when the thickness is disregarded. If the same leaf is twisted and parts of it are turned in or out, the two-dimensional form is immediately transformed into a three-dimensional figure.

EXERCISE: Using the figures in row B, create a series of three-dimensional figures.

PLATE 8

row B

PLATE 8, continued

P L A T E   9 .   On the whole, the drawings in this plate are quite realistic. They are simplified but retain many of the natural characteristics of the birds.

The compositions are complete, with the addition of plant forms with which the birds are naturally associated.

The association between a natural form and its surroundings suggests a further way in which to study source material for transformation into design.

Very often the natural association between a bird and its surroundings is changed. The change may be fantastic and shock the sensitivities of a naturalist, but it may turn out to be very good design, and that is what counts most to the designer. Besides, the designer has the power to create a world of his own in which controlled imagination plays a powerful rôle.

However, having said this, the designer must realize that he must know about things, a very great variety of things. Generally speaking, the more he knows, the more tools he has at his command to aid him in giving full play to his imagination, intuition and creative talents.

E X E R C I S E :   Combine bird and plant forms. Be aware of the over-all contours. Control them. Have definite shapes in mind.

N O T E :   The over-all shapes of the design in Plate 9 are more or less:
        (A) Rectangular ;
        (B), (E), (H) Triangular;
        (C), (D), (F), (J) Elliptical;
        (G) Circular.
These are only rough approximations of the contours but indicate a general shape.

B

A

P L A T E   9

C

D

E

F

H

G

J

PLATE 9, continued

P L A T E   1 0 .   In this plate, birds and geometric figures have been combined to create designs.

OBSERVATION: Since the bird is the most important part of each design, the background, the geometric part, must be of lesser importance but must have some of the character of the main part.

For instance, in Figure J, the bird is treated as a free form, and the same treatment is used in the background.

In Figures H and K, the angular treatment of the birds is retained in the subordinate parts.

Examine the remaining designs for union between birds and backgrounds and remember that every part of a design is important, although the parts are not of equal importance.

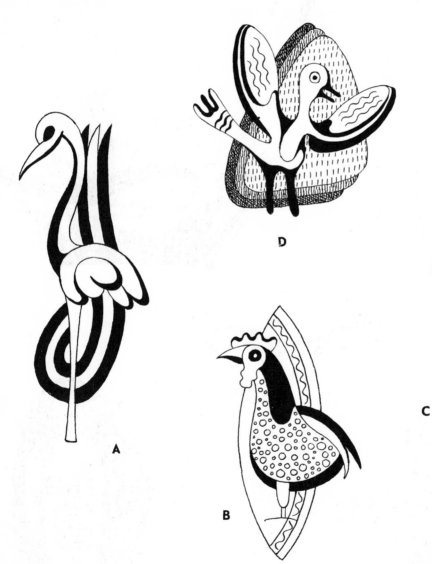

A

D

C

B

PLATE 10

E

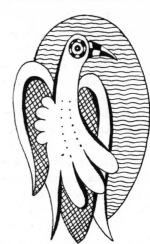

F

G

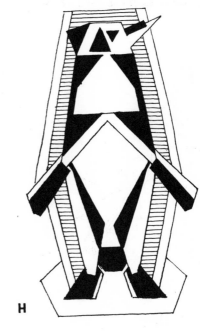

H

J

K

PLATE 10, continued

P L A T E   11.   The relationship between rounded and cubic forms is a very intimate one, artistically as well as mathematically. When the number of sides or faces of any one of the birds illustrated in Plate 11 is increased, the general effect of the form as a whole takes on a more rounded appearance, and a point is reached, theoretically at any rate, when the cubic form and the rounded form become one and the same thing.

Any sculptor working in marble, granite, or wood is well aware of this. Many ceramic sculptors build their large forms by putting together simple block forms. Then by cutting, scraping, and sand-papering they increase the number of plane surfaces. The rounding off of the corners and edges comes last and belongs to the finishing touches.

What is perhaps more important than anything else for the craftsman, the sculptor, the architect, the industrial designer, and the painter is the development of a sense of form. This can be achieved not only by observing natural and man-made form but by studying the properties of the basic geometric solids and surfaces.

The basic geometric solids are easier to draw and easier to commit to memory than the infinitely more complex forms of nature. It is for these reasons that a very good way of studying animal, bird, and human form is to find the simplest geometric shapes that will most nearly conform to the realistic figures. Where this has been done, the plane surfaces are sub-divided until the rounded forms begin to take shape.

P L A T E   11

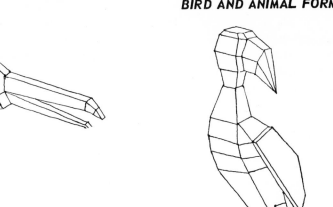

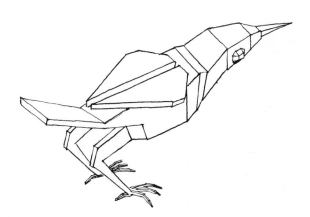

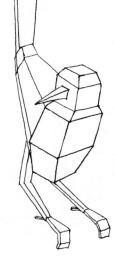

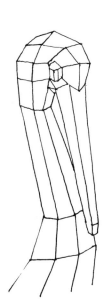

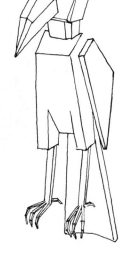

P L A T E 11 , continued

PLATE 12. In this plate, free-form animal figures have been used to create the various compositions shown.

The plane free-form is comparatively easy to draw and can therefore be very useful to the designer for putting down ideas with a minimum of effort. For those who are weak in drawing, it offers a way of self-expression that is not too inhibiting.

PLATE 12

PLATE 12, *continued*

P L A T E   1 3 .   For the most part, the animal figures have been treated quite realistically.

This was done for three principal reasons:

(1) Even though each individual part may be realistic, the assembly can be arranged to produce ordered design by controlling the flow of line and the areas of interest.

(2) The extent to which a design may be good or bad does not depend upon the amount of distortion, simplification, or any other type of treatment which alters the forms used.

(3) In all the other illustrations based on animal form, I have used a considerable amount of distortion and simplification to produce the designs. We must not rule out realism.

The truth of the matter is that any form of art, whether expressionistic, surrealistic, or anything else, does not guarantee that the result will be good design. Mediocrity plays no favorites. It occurs too often in every movement, and if the designer, the man himself, doesn't amount to much, his work, whatever devices he uses, will not attain a high level.

E X E R C I S E : Create a series of compositions using two or more figures:
   (1) Realistic figures.
   (2) Simplified (outline principally).
   (3) Abstract figures.

PLATE 13

P L A T E 13, continued

P L A T E   14 .   This plate features a group of designs combining animal and human forms in which the animal forms are dominant.

If you will compare the variations in this group with those in the chapter on flower and plant form, you will note that, aside from subject matter, practically the same approach has been used:

(1) Definite contour shapes.

(2) Conformity in character between the dominant and sub-dominant parts.

(3) Simplifications of the figures without eliminating all semblance of reality.

The amount of realism or abstraction employed by the designer is a personal matter. He works as he thinks best, as his conception of the fitness of things dictates, and as his technical mastery will permit.

N O T E :   Figure 6 is symmetrical about a vertical axis. It is one of the comparatively few symmetrical designs that I have created in this work. One reason for the inclusion of very little on symmetric design is the comparative simplicity with which it is created. Once the basic notion is grasped, that of repetition about an axis, the rest follows. A second reason is the greater interest that asymmetric design holds because of the greater variety of spaces. A third reason is that the evolution of asymmetric design is a greater challenge to the imagination of the designer.

1.

2.

3.

4.

5.

6.

P L A T E   14,   *continued*

PLATE 15. This plate illustrates the use of thin prismatic forms in the creation of three-dimensional animal shapes. The prisms may also be used to build plant, bird, human, and other kinds of shapes.

<u>The basic shape is the prism.</u> All the surfaces, and the proportions of length, width, and height may be varied as one sees fit.

<u>When the basic shape is changed to the cylindric, by bending</u>, at least two of the surfaces are cylindric surfaces.

NOTE: Consult chapter on geometric form.

<u>When the basic shape is changed by twisting</u>, we get helical surfaces.

Basically, both the prismatic and cylindric surfaces may be twisted.

The combination of the three different surfaces offers many possibilities for interesting three dimensional design.

NOTE: In Plate 15, the twisted form is used in the neck of the giraffe. Practically all the other surfaces in each of the designs are plane or cylindric surfaces.

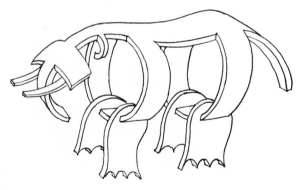

PLATE 15

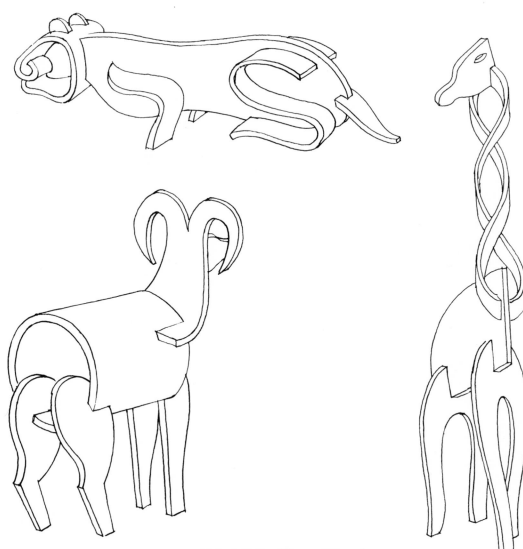

PLATE 15, continued

P L A T E   16 .   In Plate 16, figures 1, 2, and 3 have the same type of surfaces as the figures of Plate 15.   Figures 4, 5, and 6 are composed of more rounded masses, principally cylinders, elongated cones, partial spheres, and partial toroids.

N O T E :   Refer to surfaces and solids in the chapter on geometric form.

The combination of thin wire forms and the heavier solid masses gives Figures 4, 5, and 6 more variety and interest. Various parts of the figures are treated differently to emphasize in different degrees the heads, torsos, or legs.

The author is well aware of the fact that there is a vast difference between a drawing of a three-dimensional figure and the figure itself. Very often the drawing has to be modified and the original conception changed to make construction possible. If changes have to be made, consider them a challenge that has to be met. Anyone who has ever done anything in design knows the difficulties that have to be overcome so that the finished product will conform as nearly as possible to the basic idea.

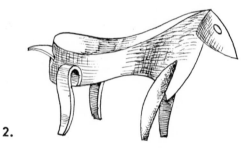

2.

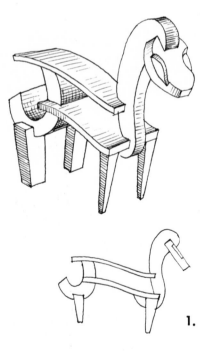

1.

PLATE 16

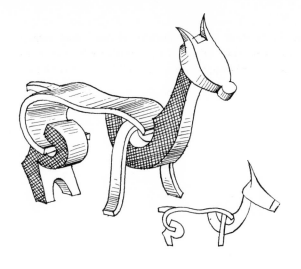

3.

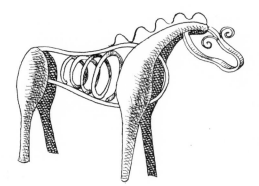

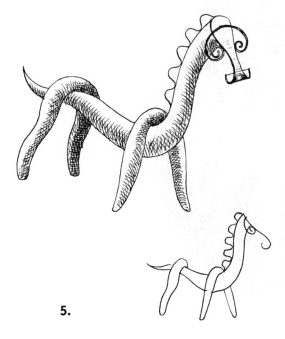

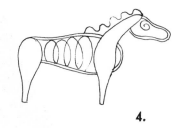

4.

5.

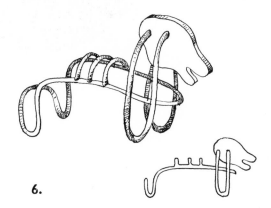

6.

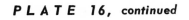

P L A T E   16, continued

PLATE 17.   The designs in Plate 17 feature a combination of bird and human forms in which the bird forms are dominant. The problems that arise in connection with the combinations used here are similar to those in which various elements were assembled, as illustrated in the other chapters.

PLATE 17

P L A T E   17, continued

P L A T E   18.   In this plate three-dimensional representations of the bird are composed principally of plane and cylindric surfaces.

The principal divisions of the natural form must be kept in mind so that mental concepts can be built. The special interests of each designer play a very important part in creating design. A sculptor working with such materials as marble or granite will think in terms of bulk-weight forms, while a metal craftsman, working with comparatively thin sheets of metal, will think in terms of ribbon forms.

The mistake that artists, craftsmen, and designers very often make is that of narrowing their interests, shutting out everything that doesn't have an immediate tie-in with what they are doing. They do not realize the full importance of the intimate relationship between thinking and creating in all media. Furthermore, they do not appreciate that all problems of transformation into design contain elements that are two and three-dimensional.

EXERCISE 1. Design three-dimensional birds using spherical and cylindrical forms.

EXERCISE 2. Design three-dimensional birds using combination of rounded and plane surfaces.

PLATE 18

PLATE 18, continued

P L A T E   1 9 .   This plate illustrates the use of rounded solids as the equivalents of the various parts of the natural form.

Compare with Plate 11 of this chapter and note the differences between cubic and rounded forms.

In Plate 19, the bird has been subdivided into beak, head, neck, body, and leg, and each part has been treated with a simplicity that suggests in a general way the essential character of the part.

This approach may be used in dealing with any of the natural forms.

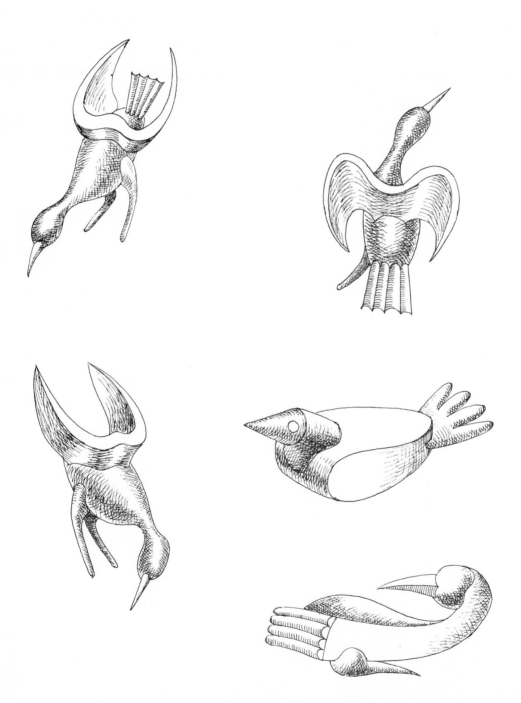

P L A T E   19

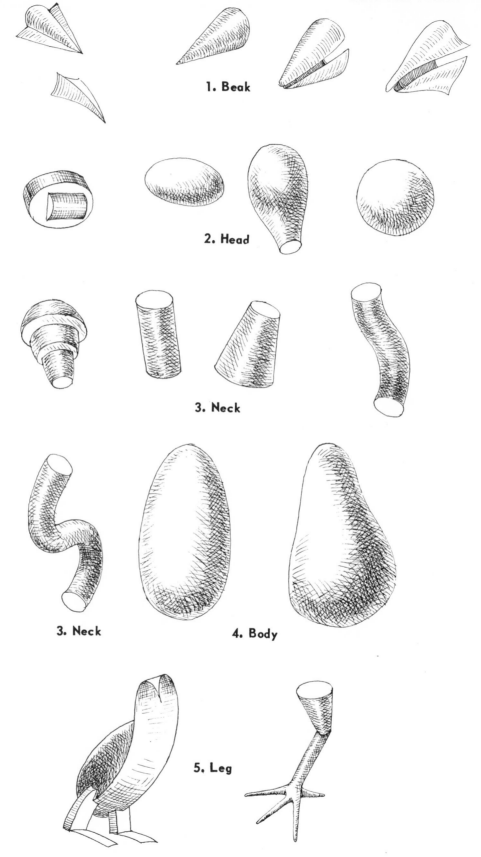

1. Beak

2. Head

3. Neck

3. Neck   4. Body

5. Leg

PLATE 19, continued

MAN-MADE FORM

A. Introduction

B. Plates:

INTRODUCTION

The average human being does not have the sensitivity of the designer. The former is only dimly conscious of the many different shapes and colors that he sees in his daily living. It is only something striking that makes him stop and look. The designer, average though he may be in other respects, is keenly aware of the things around him and sensitive to the shapes and colors that surround him.

I am talking about such common objects as buildings, automobiles, chairs, telephones, spoons, door knobs, musical instruments, and all other man-made things that we see and use. These objects are part of our very existence, and the changes that are continually taking place in their shapes, colors, and materials, reflect, among other things, the influence of art in our daily living.

Sometimes, as in the case of the automobile, the change in design over a very few years has been startling. This is also true of modern interior design for homes and offices. We see new, strange, almost weird looking television aerials. They are helping to change the landscape, and I am sure that before long there will be wallpaper and textile designs that will use these new forms.

Man-made things are functional. They are made to be used. The student of design must take function into account when he studies the general make-up of the object as a whole. He must become aware of the shapes, the interplay of different surfaces, the dominant flow of line, the various textures of the materials used, and combinations of colors. Sometimes the colors are accidental, as in the case of a row of houses subject to exposure to the elements.

Since man-made objects are inanimate and very often predominantly geometric, a study of their shapes and essential lines can be combined with a study of geometric forms.

Texture can best be studied by going to the objects themselves for reference and then experimenting with varieties of shapes, using the textures seen and touched, and then deliberately creating out of different materials the same shapes and surfaces.

Texture undoubtedly plays an important part in design, but its importance can be overplayed and over-exaggerated. Materials are used for two principal reasons; namely, aesthetic and structural. The structural fitness can be determined in a laboratory, and the element of chance can be completely eliminated.

The aesthetic aspect of the problem is not so easily solved. Its evaluation cannot as yet be precisely made.

A third reason for the use of materials is purely economic. Availability or ease of manufacture are very often the determining factors in making a choice. When the question arises as to a choice between wood or plastic, brick or stone, for the sake of appearance, there we leave the laboratory and enter into the realm of feeling, instinct, and intuition. We may be dogmatic about the choice we make, but we cannot prove that we are right. It may not be necessary to prove that we are right, but we must not be so sure of ourselves that we lose sight of the fact that there are other solutions which may be equally good or better.

Man-made forms offer a wide variety of subject matter that can be of great use to the designer if he will observe them carefully, study them, and use them as basic source material.

P L A T E   1 .   The source is part of a casting having a shape somewhat like a bottle.

Consider Figures A, B, and C.   The three motifs represent parts of the object and are considered as distinct units after they have been separated from the source.

Each of the three motifs is linear and two-dimensional and has been repeated to form a running pattern.

B and C are repeated along a horizontal line.

A has been repeated along a horizontal and a vertical axis, forming a unit composed of four A's.   This unit has been repeated along a vertical line.

In Figure D, surfaces have been abstracted from the source and combined to form a new three-dimensional object.   The design used plane, cylindric, and toroidal surfaces.

Figure E.   A free transformation keeping the three-dimensional figure, as a whole, cylindric in feeling.

Figures F, G, H.   These are two-dimensional compositions whose areas of chief interest are derived from the lines and surfaces in the source and form the basis for a development into a complete design.

N O T E :   In Figures A, B, C, and D repeat lines have been added to give a sense of completeness to each arrangement.

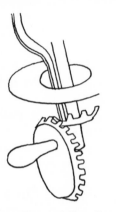

Part of Egg Beater

Folding Chair

Part of Lighting Fixture

E X E R C I S E :   Use the above man-made objects as the basis for design.

A

A₁

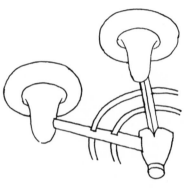

B₁

B

C₁

C

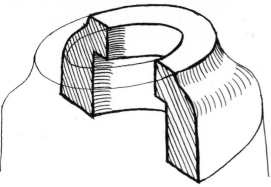

C2

D

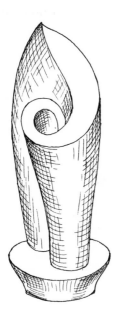

F

E

G

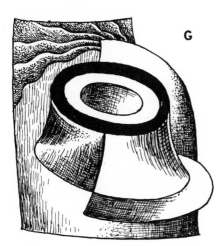

H

PLATE 1

P L A T E 2 . This plate is composed entirely of source material. The violin is seen in its entirety from one angle, and various parts of it are also shown. Many different views of the elements are possible, and any attempt at an exhaustive investigation would lead to a very large accumulation of source material for design.

It is important for the designer to realize this because very often he spends a lot of time and effort searching for new material when it is at hand, if only he will make full use of it.

I happen to like music and musical instruments very much and have used them many times in creating two and three-dimensional design. If your tastes run to other things, then by all means, select the source material you are interested in. Whatever it may be, study it, draw it, take it apart, record all of it, and then begin to create.

E X E R C I S E S :

(1) Study the relationship of the various planes.
(2) Study different types of surfaces.
(3) Make three-dimensional models of the various parts (paper, wood, soap, clay). Simplify the very complex parts.
(4) Put the segments together in different orders.

P L A T E 2

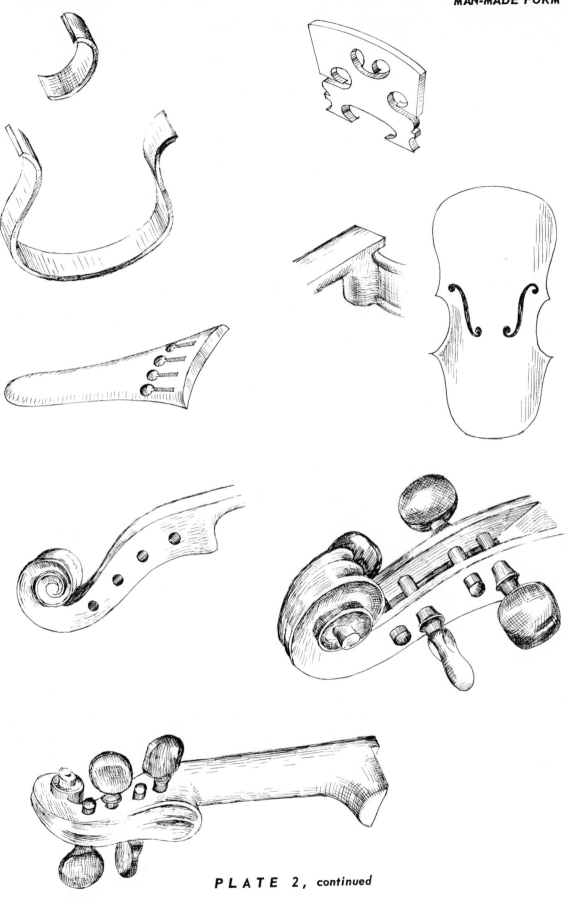

PLATE 2, continued

P L A T E   3 .   Designs based on material in **Plate 2.**

Row **A** in **Plate 3** shows seven three-dimensional designs based on **Figure 2.** Each is a combination of plane and cylindric surfaces. This is an illustration of how the same plane view may be interpreted to represent many different space objects.

Row **C** in **Plate 3** shows two-dimensional designs that are more involved than **Figure 1** in Row **A.**

E X E R C I S E : Make three-dimensional interpretations of each. (Draw, model in soap, clay or plaster).

E X A M P L E :

Designs based on fig-
ures in row C, Plate 3.

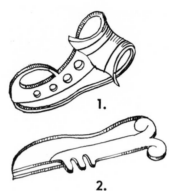

1.

2.

3.

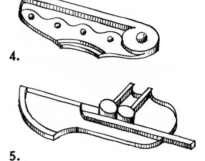

4.

5.

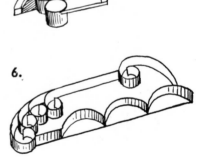

7.

6.

Row **B** in **Plate 3** represents abstract two-dimensional compositions. The themes are derived from the source material in **Plate 2.**

The compositions were inspired by the rhythms (flow of line) in the object itself and represent a considerable amount of freedom of interpretation. Incidentally, the final design very often will not resemble the object from which it is created. The main purpose of the source is to serve as a starting point.

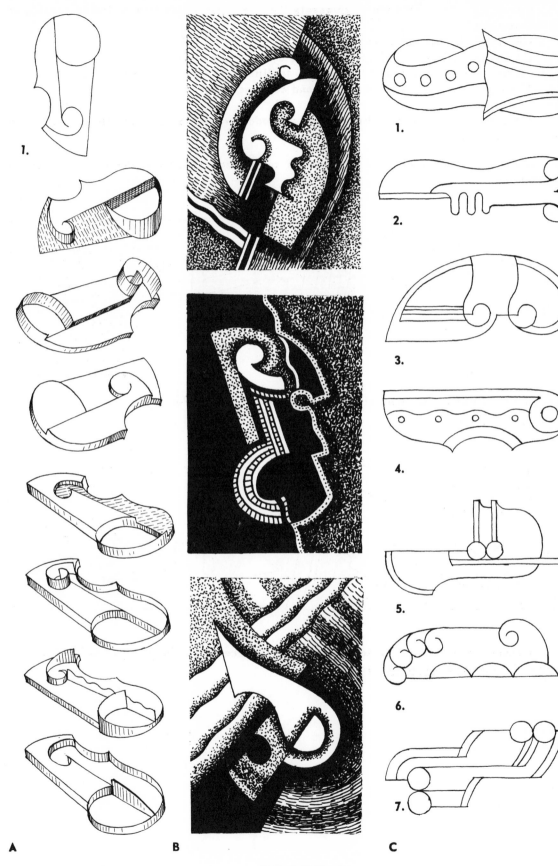

A   B   C

PLATE 3

P L A T E 4 . This plate represents the use of man-made form which is considered to be transparent.

The figures in horizontal row A show:

(1) The realistic set-up of a table, a box, a bowl, and a glass.

(2) Heavy lines show two of the many quite different contours which are part of the set-up.

The figures in row B show the areas and contours clearly defined and separated from the group.

Figures in row C: Repeat lines have been added to the black and white values to complete the compositions.

N O T E : Keep objects simple when in combination; otherwise, there is apt to be too much confusion.

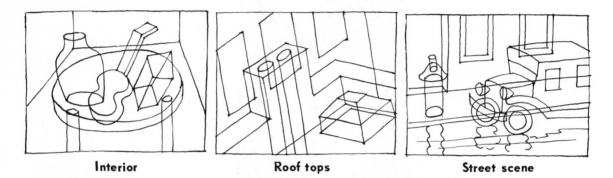

| Interior | Roof tops | Street scene |

E X E R C I S E : Use material above as realistic bases for design.

E X A M P L E :

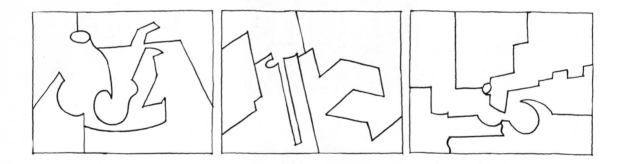

Complete compositions, using auxiliary lines if necessary. Create other compositions by using the given material <u>as well as</u> your own.

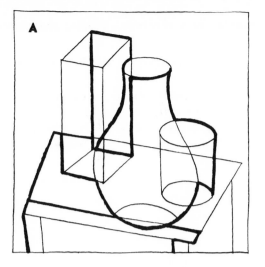

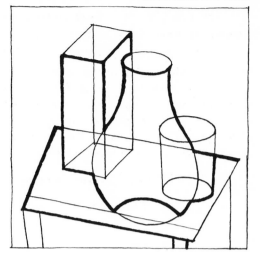

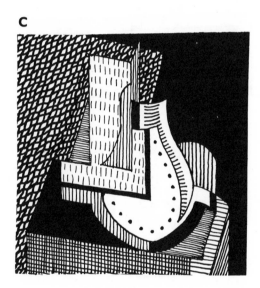

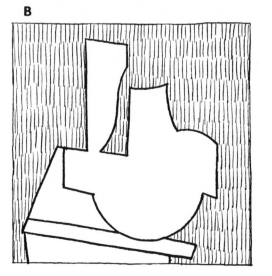

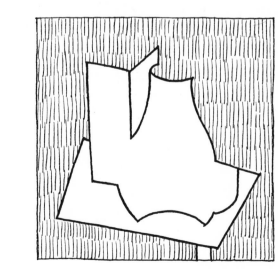

PLATE 4

PLATE 5. In this plate, study the examples very carefully, keeping the source material in front of you so that you can compare the two.

The rhythms, in the drawings made on the spot, are determined by the flow of line and the space relationship of the various parts.

For example, look at Figures 4 and 8. The subject matter is very much the same in each drawing, but the combinations of lines and areas are quite different. In Figure 8, the vertical lines of the piles are very important while in Figure 4, the curved line formed by the lines of the boats flowing into the lines of the wharf is striking. The designs based on the two realistic drawings reflect the different rhythmic features of the originals.

EXERCISE: Create designs based on source material.

EXAMPLES:

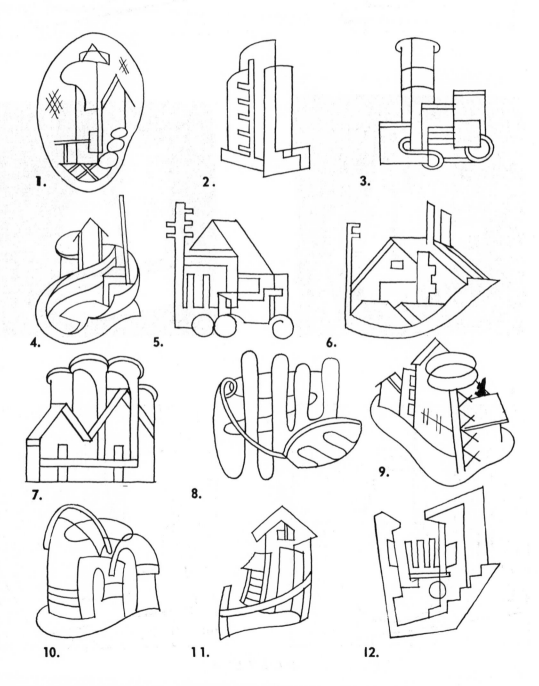

1.   2.   3.

4.   5.   6.

7.   8.   9.

10.   11.   12.

1.

2.

3.

4.

5.

6.

7.

8.

9.

10.

11.

12.

PLATE 5

PLATE 6. Sketch of a street scene in Catskill, N.Y. Of course, this subject is not exclusively man-made because of the clouds, the sky, and the trees, but since they play an unimportant role in the composition, they may be disregarded.

There is a tremendous amount of material, man-made, which is most useful for design.

(1) Industrial (factory buildings, machinery).
(2) Travel (bus, streetcar, plane, boat).
(3) Amusement (circus, fair-grounds, musical instruments).
(4) Household (telephone, egg beater, chair).
(5) Street and harbor scenes (buildings, boats).

The list above will do for a start.

Each category can be divided into hundreds of components. The subject matter is inexhaustible and also readily available. All you need is your sketchbook.

The important thing is to collect material and learn about it. It is not necessary to pay too much attention to composition when in search of facts. Many artists and designers frankly admit that they cannot compose out-of-doors.

EXERCISE: How many motifs can you find in Plate 6?

PLATE 6

PLATE 7. This represents six variations based on the street scene in Plate 6. In no one of them have I departed very far from realism.

(1) The order in which the various parts occur in the sketch has been changed.

(2) In B and C, which are more abstract than any of the others, the controlled flow of line and placement of the lights and darks have changed the general design.

Except in Figure D, where some curvature is shown, angularity has been stressed by using straight lines.

It would have been just as possible for me to emphasize angularity by using combinations of straight and curved lines. However, the character of the composition would then have been changed.

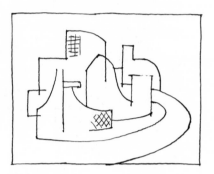

EXERCISES: Go back to Plate 6. It is the source material.

(1) Create compositions, using straight and curved lines.

(2) Create compositions, using all curved lines.

(3) Do this with the material in Plates 5 and 8.

A

B

C

D

E

F

PLATE 7

PLATE 8.   Compositions based on a Gloucester boat scene. In each example the relationships between the various parts in the drawing from nature are carried out.

EXERCISE: Use your own source material to create a series of compositions.

EXERCISE: Separate the various units that compose the original and rearrange them to form new designs.

EXAMPLE:

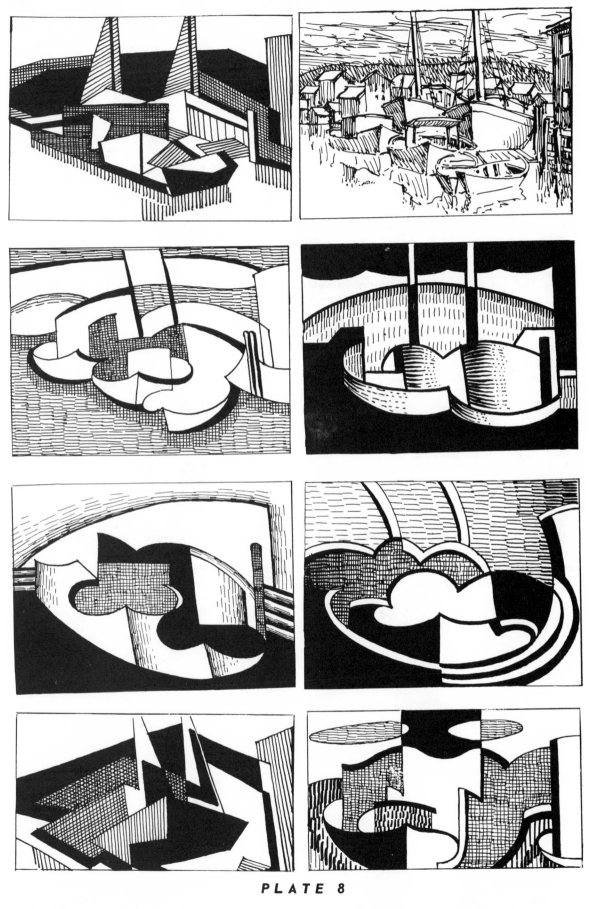

PLATE 8

PLATE 9. This plate shows how a partial interior view and a partial exterior view may be combined to form a composition.

The composition is divided into two principal parts:

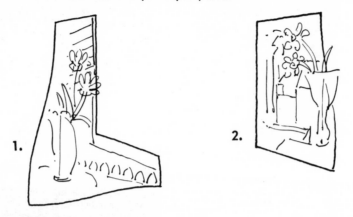

The two parts, while different in subject matter, are united by repetition of the same motif in each part.

They are also united by a continuous flow of line from Part 1 to Part 2, and the similar treatment of the leaves and flowers. The repetition thus used helps to unite what might otherwise become two unrelated parts.

Part 2 as a whole is more dominant than Part 1.

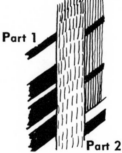

A safe rule to follow in working out any composition is to make one part of the work more important, more eye-catching, than the rest. If this is done, everything else in the arrangement may be of equal value. If there is no dominant element, there will be too many parts claiming the attention of the observer simultaneously. This will lead to confusion.

NOTE: Basically, the arrangement in this plate illustrates the same principle as Plate 4 in chapter on composition.

PLATE 9

P L A T E   1 0 .   The four compositions in Plate 10 are entitled:

(1) Painting the Bridge.

(2) Fishermen's Shacks, Rockport.

(3) Street Scene, New York

(4) From the Terrace.

In composition 1, the tendency for the eye to move in the direction of the converging lines is offset by the very important figure which is of chief interest.

In composition 2, the dominant areas are connected by part of a boat and part of the net. While most of the lines are straight lines, curved ones are also important. This adds a type of variety which does not occur in any of the other compositions in this plate.

N O T E :   The use of curved and straight lines in a design does not make it a better or worse design than one using either all straight or all curved lines. It just makes it different.

The power of line is such that we can use it to give expression to the many different emotions, feelings, or moods we may wish to illustrate. Each designer must decide for himself what kind of line will best express the particular idea he has in mind.

In composition 3, there is considerable stylization of the street and buildings which make up the principal part of the picture. The automobile is of chief interest, and the human figures have been drawn so as to conform with the spirit of the rest of the composition. (This represents the principle of conformity which plays a very important part in many types of design).

Composition 4, just as composition 3, illustrates the principle of conformity and its use. Note the similarity but not the sameness of general prismatic shapes of buildings. Note the importance of the sloping lines. Note how the contrasts of light and dark are used throughout the picture.

Repetition is a type of conformity generally less complex because identical forms and parallelism are used.

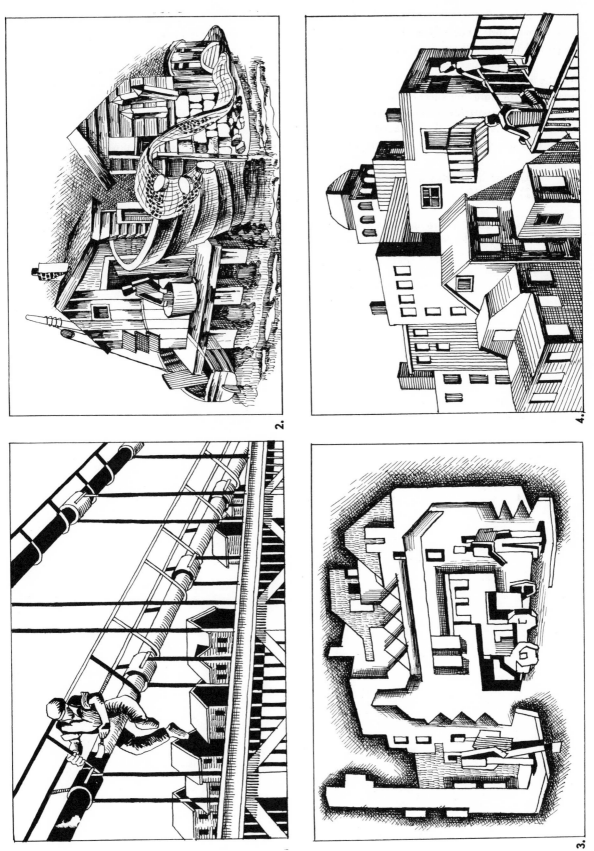

2.

4.

3.

P L A T E   10

PLATE 11. Plate 11 might very well have been assigned to the chapter on plant and animal form, but since the boats and net are man-made and play a conspicuous role in the design, I felt that there was sufficient reason for including the plate in this chapter.

This composition has been devised so that it can be repeated to form an all-over pattern. As the single composition is viewed and studied, it is definitely one thing, and our reaction to it based on its solo appearance, will be quite different from our reaction when we see it repeated. As soon as repetition is introduced, the theme, as you now see it, has neighbors added to it, and it is the neighbors that make the difference.

In creating the all-over pattern or design, two of the most important problems to consider are:

(1) The basic design.
(2) The effect on the basic design by repetition.

NOTE: There are many important practical problems attached to design of this type which come under the heading of textile design.

PLATE 11

SECTION FIVE

HUMAN FORM

INTRODUCTION

When we design or compose, it is never done with complete detachment. There is always an emotional response to the source material we use, and there is always the injection of emotion into the things we wish to say and the way we say them. The outcome will be a work which may be coldly objective or will express violent emotion. Between the two extremes, there can be any number of intermediate results, and each one of them will express in some degree the feelings and aims of the designer. The success or failure of the creation will depend upon the degree to which it measures up to the intention of the artist. This measure of accomplishment deals only with the relationship between the designer and his work and has nothing to do with the reactions of anyone else.

The creative designer grows in his powers to express himself as his technique improves, as his ideas take shape and emerge from obscurity, and as he develops a greater critical faculty for judging the relative degree to which his works conform to his ideas.

In other words, the designer knows when he is wanting in any phase of his work. No one has to tell the artist that he does not know how to draw the human figure or that his lack of knowledge of human anatomy reveals his ignorance of it. He knows it only too well, and if he is sincere and earnest in his desire for self-improvement, he will do something definite about it.

The designer must be his own severest critic. This is more easily said than done, but it must be done sooner or later.

Specifically, how much human anatomy should be studied? There can be no blanket answer that will satisfactorily cover all cases. Much depends upon the degree to which memory has been developed to recall shapes, action, and function. Obviously some designers have to work harder and longer than others to acquire the same knowledge and skills.

The minimum requirement, in my judgment, is a study which will equip the artist with :

    (1) A knowledge of the fundamental shapes of the figure as a whole and its major components.

    (2) A knowledge of the bone and muscle structure with special attention to function and effect on visible shapes and contours.

    (3) Effect of distortion, due to bending and twisting, on the relative proportions of the major parts of the figure.

    (4) A study of the relationship between the realistic shapes of the figure and geometric counterparts.

This knowledge can best be attained by drawing and observation of the live human figure, by study of anatomy as related to the artist's point of view, and by making three dimensional models of the figure and its parts. The model-making should be undertaken simultaneously with the other technical work.

Such an outline of study as I have proposed will be a long step in the right direction. Of itself, it will not answer all of your needs. It is hardly more than a beginning. What you do with it and the extent to which it will enable you to expand your powers of expressions will depend upon your natural endowments and the sincerity and perseverance with which you employ them.

P L A T E   1 .   Horizontal row A of Plate 1 shows four simplified drawings of the human figure in action. This type of drawing, which is sometimes called 'stick figure', is very effective for two main reasons. First, it indicates the action of the figure; and second, it helps establish the general character of the figure; that is, whether the figure will be short or tall thin or stout. (Relative widths and lengths of the major part of the figure.)

Here are a few illustrations to show the general character:

Don't expect too much from this kind of simple drawing, but it can be extremely useful. Rows B, C, and D show various ways in which the stick figures are filled out.

| Head | Torso | Hips | Arms | Legs | Head | Torso | Arms | Legs |

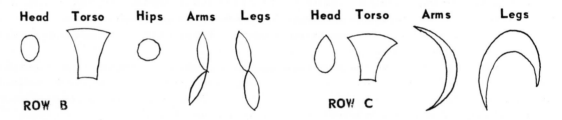

ROW B   ROW C

Row D shows the filled out figure as a free form. While the major divisions of the figure are recognizable, there is no separation of the parts.

Other ways of filling out the figure are by the use of all straight lines or a combination of of straight and curved lines.

E X A M P L E :

ROW A Fig. 1.

E X E R C I S E S: (1) Draw many simple skeletonized (stick) figures showing different action.

(2) Fill out figures by methods shown.

(3) Create a series of designs by rearranging the various parts of the figure.

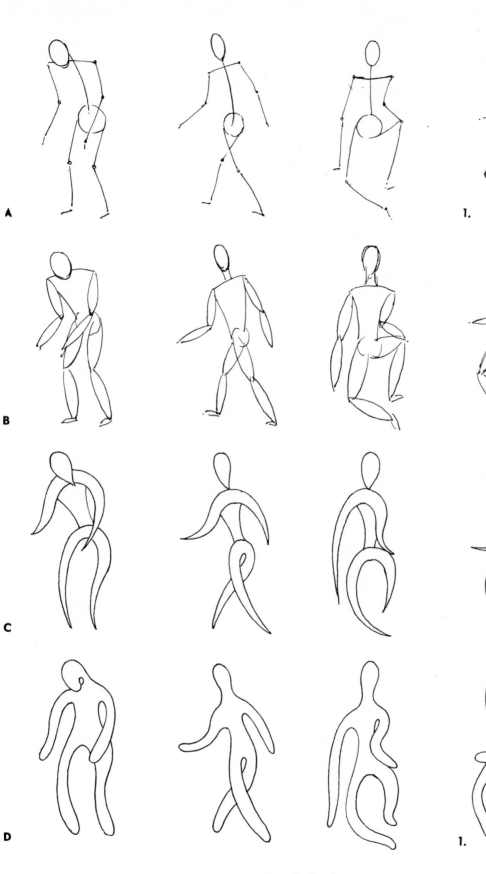

A

B

C

D

1.

1.

PLATE 1

PLATE 2.   In this plate, all of the designs were derived from the drawing of the crouching figure in the upper right corner of Plate 2.

In most of the variations, the action has been retained. Figures 2, 4, 5, and 7 show the the greatest departure, as far as action is concerned.

It is almost impossible to speak of the 'simplest geometric equivalent' in such a complex form as our source material. There are a number of simple equivalents, and your choice will be a matter of personal reaction. A great deal depends upon the impression you get at some given time. When you come back to the figure later, you may see it in an entirely different way and a different set of lines will impress itself upon you. The result of such a change of interest will show in the lines and shapes that you use to begin your design.

2. Extreme contours

1. Skeletal figure

Curved lines   **Straight lines**   **Curved and straight lines**

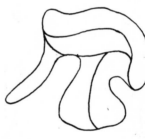

3. Extreme and inner contours

4. Extreme and human contours   **5. Extreme contour**   **6. Extreme and human contours**
                                          greatly simplified

1.

2.

3.

4.

5.

6.

7.

8.

9.

10.

11.

12.

PLATE 2

PLATE 3.

(1) Simplify each of the ten figures according to the suggestions in Plates 1 and 2.

(2) Use black, white, and intermediate values.

(3) Assemble figures in groups of two or more to form compositions.   Extreme contour of group should be a geometric figure, such as a rectangle, circle, or triangle.

(4) Consider figures transparent (if it will help your design).

(5) Change relative sizes and positions of figures to suit.

(6) Repeat figures if necessary.

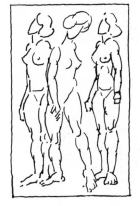

Figure 9, Figure 2, repeated

Figures 4, 3, 10, 6, 7, 9.
(Figure 3 reversed and altered)

Figures 7, 8, 5, 1.

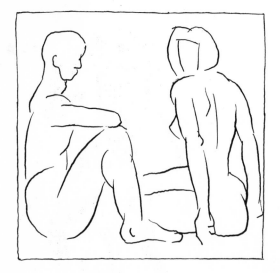

Figures 3, 6

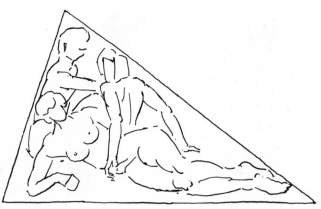

Figures 5, 6, 3

PLATE 3

PLATE 4. When two or more figures form the basic source material, each figure may be considered separately and then the two or more united. This will mean creating two or more fundamental forms. When united, the fundamental forms or extreme contours may then be simplified to make a single fundamental form expressive of the whole.

Fig. B in Plate 4 considered as a unit.   Fig. B in Plate 4 treated as two separate units.

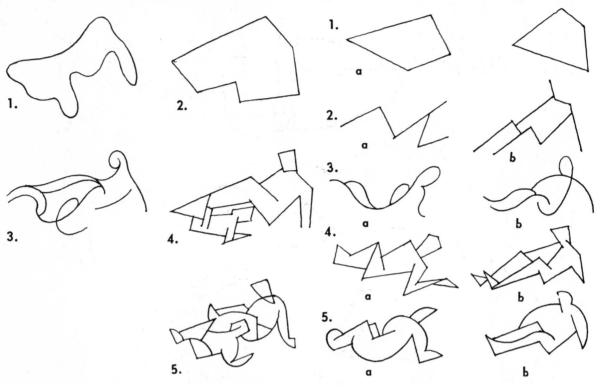

In examples 3, 4, 5, we have in each instance, a composite. We may complete the design by enclosing it within a pre-arranged shape, such as a rectangle, circle, or triangle, or create an asymmetric contour, in which the figures will be contained.

We now have two sets of distinctly different interpretations of the natural forms, and we may put them together in any order that suits our purpose.

EXAMPLES:

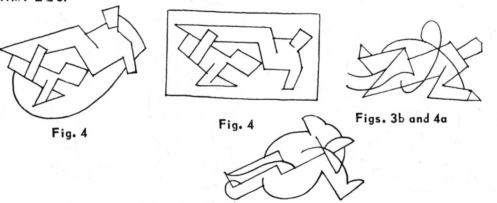

Fig. 4   Fig. 4   Figs. 3b and 4a

Figs. 5a and 5b

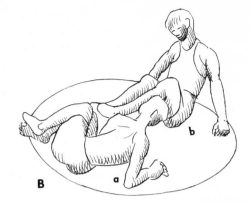

A

B

b

a

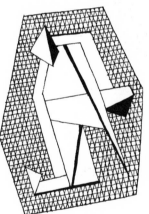

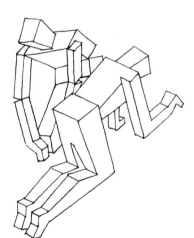

PLATE 4

PLATE 5. Figure A in Plate 5 is the realistic representation of human form. Enough shading has been used to give the figure solidity.

Figure B represents the human figure simplified by substituting plane surfaces for the rounded forms. The total figure becomes a composite of cubes, rectangular blocks, truncated pyramids, and prisms.

Figure C. Rounded shapes, much simpler than in Figure A, made up the human form. The ellipsoid, the sphere, the torus, the cylinder, and the cone and parts thereof are the principal solids used.

The complexity or simplicity of the design will depend upon the extent to which the figure is altered by planes or curved surfaces.

Figure B1. has fewer planes than Figure B.

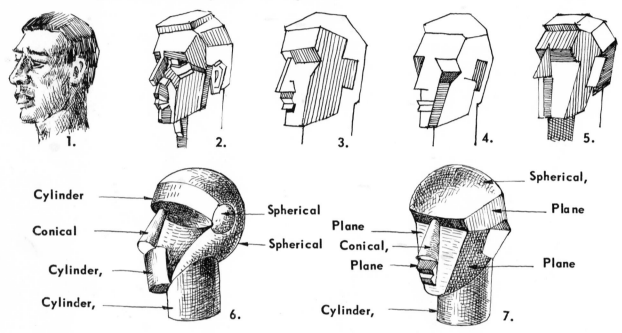

EXERCISE: Use the figures of Plate 3 as source material. Convert into block forms as in Figure B and into rounded forms as in Figure C.

EXERCISE: Use combinations of block and rounded forms. Figure 7 illustrates the use of plane and rounded surfaces to create new heads.

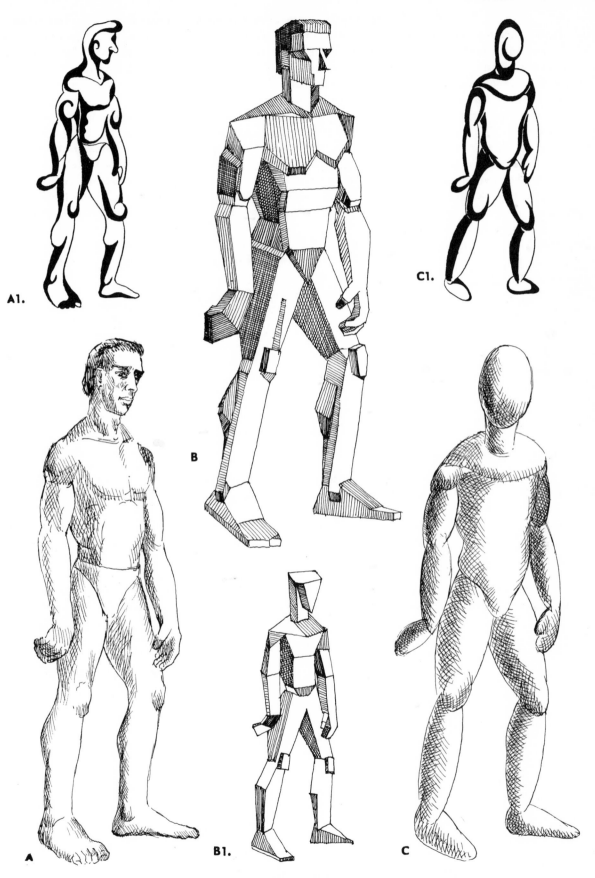

A1.

B

C1.

A

B1.

C

PLATE 5

PLATE 6 .   The figures in Plate 6 show what the human form looks like when it is drawn using cubic blocks. All of the surfaces of the naturally rounded areas have been converted into plane surfaces. There is nothing new about this method of representing the figure. Albrecht Dürer did it more than four hundred years ago. Many of the modern painters, beginning with Cezanne, gave new life to art by exploring the possibilities inherent in this approach to a rendition of form.

The importance of seeing and drawing immensely complex figures, both human and animal, in this way, lies in the fact that it is a process of simplification. At first glance, you may not think that it is simple at all, but when you compare it with the attempt at rendering the host of subtly curved surfaces of the natural object, you will realize what the difference is. Another important reason for practising the drawing of bird, animal, and human figures in this way is that you develop definite simple, mental images of the various parts of the body. When these images become fixed in your mind, the drawing of any figure, whatever its position, becomes easier.

1. Each major part of the figure, 1. head, 2. neck, 3. torso, 4. arms, 5. legs, 6. hands, and 7. feet, has a more or less characteristic shape. Decide what the shape is. Use the figures below as a guide for starting.

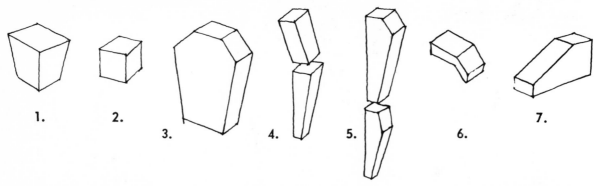

1.   2.   3.   4.   5.   6.   7.

As you become accustomed to these shapes, and when you have drawn them in different positions, make models out of soap, clay or plasticene, and put them together to resemble the human figure.

After gaining some mastery in handling the very simple forms, make them more complicated by going back to the natural figures and studying them for details, such as nose, knee-cap, toes, etc.

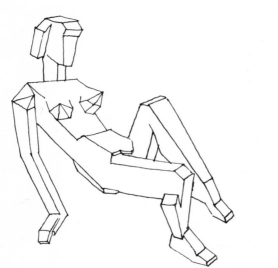
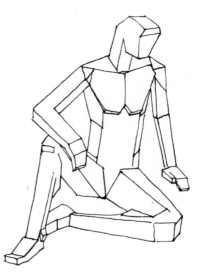

PLATE 6

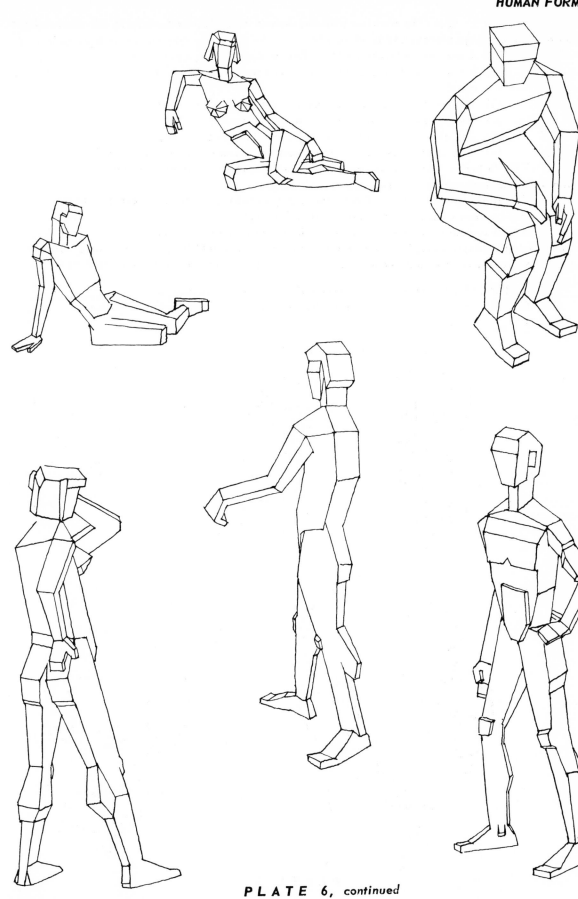

PLATE 6, continued

PLATE 7. In working with the human head, as well as with all other natural material, the design process starts when:

    (1) A part or parts are omitted (Figure A).

    (2) A part or parts are changed in shape and/or size, either larger or smaller. (Figure B).

    (3) The relative positions of one or more parts are altered. (Figure C).

    (4) The extreme contours are changed. (Figure D)

    (5) The object or any of its parts is imagined to be transparent.

    (6) Two or more aspects of the object are shown in combination to form a unit.

The departure from realism depends upon the extent to which any one or any combination of the several devices is used.

The illustrations in Plate 7 are essentially two-dimensional in character. Some of them can readily be transformed into three-dimensional design.

If you are going to create space or three-dimensional design, think in terms of space from the very outset. Every line and area in your drawing should be envisioned as a representation of a space area, the intersection between two surfaces, or the contours of surfaces.

    EXERCISE: Create two-dimensional variations of source material.

    EXERCISE: Create three-dimensional variations. (Fig. 1., 2., 3. below)

    EXAMPLES:

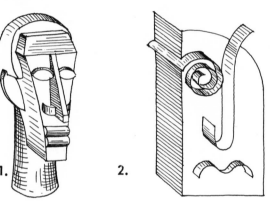

1.   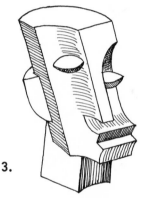   2.   3.

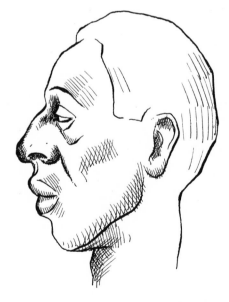

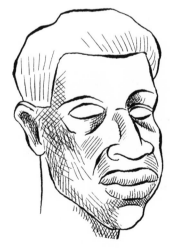

PLATE 7

PLATE 7, continued

P L A T E   8 .   In this plate the human figure is divided into separate segments as shown in Figure B.

The segments are shown as separate and distinct units in Figure C.

Figure D shows six different combinations of various segments, each group forming a different composition.

N O T E :   In some of the examples in Figure D, transition lines and repeat lines help complete the arrangements. In others, enveloping lines have been used.

E X E R C I S E S : Use Figure A. Divide the figure into segments which correspond to the natural divisions of the natural form.

        (1) (A) All straight lines.
             (B) All curves.
             (C) Combination of curves and straight lines.
        (2) Combine to form complete compositions.

N O T E :   In the beginning, disregard the small features, such as eyes, ears, etc.

        (3) Use Figure B as source. Create a series of variations.

E X A M P L E S :

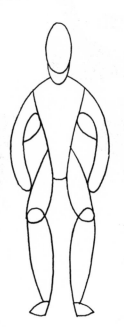
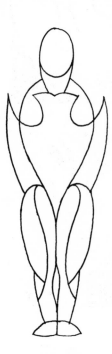
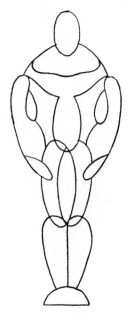

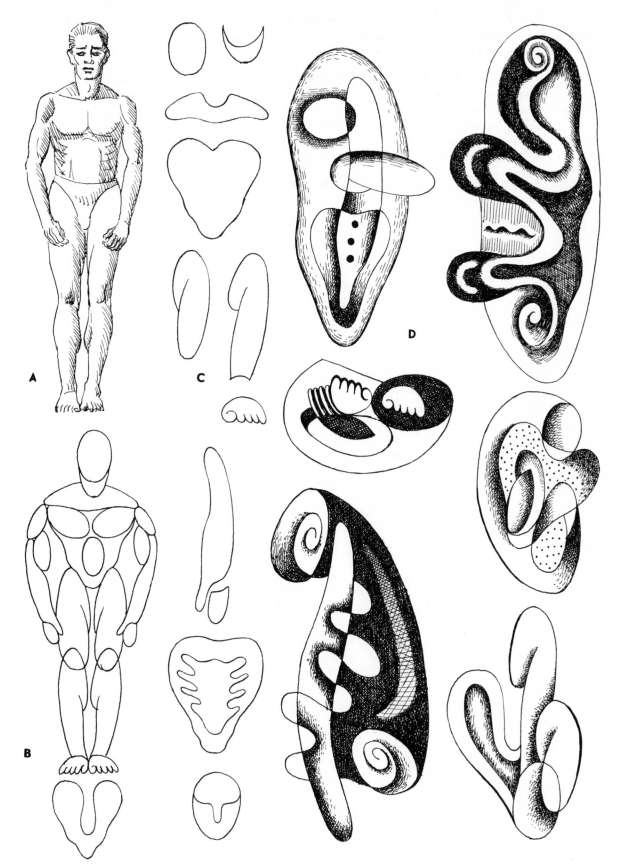

A

B

C

D

PLATE 8

PLATE 9. This plate is a combination of human and man-made material. In no one of the examples shown in Plate 9 has the departure from realism produced an abstract design which is not quite closely identified with the original source.

EXERCISE: Figure A stems from the original source and corresponds to the drawing and sketches you will make of material that interests you and that you think can be transformed into design.

Using Figure A, employ various methods suggested in Plates 2 and 4 to go from the realistic to the abstract.

NOTE: In the beginning do not make too great a jump from the source material.

EXERCISE: Create a series of designs based on a combination of human and man-made material.

EXAMPLES:

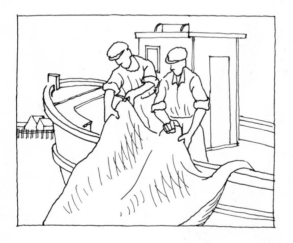

1.

2.

A

PLATE 9

P L A T E   10.   The four compositions in this plate are made up of plant, human, and man-made forms.

In each case the man-made form has been expressed with straight lines as a contrast to the flowing lines of the natural material.

E X E R C I S E S: Compose groups using two or more types of material:
         (1) All curved lines.
         (2) All straight lines.
         (3) Combinations of straight and curved lines.

N O T E: The compositions should employ the following combinations: plant and animal; plant, cloud, and mountain; plant and fish.

Very little has been said about the effect on design of the physical material used to create the design. It is obvious that working in the round, or three-dimensionally, calls for a different frame of thinking than working on a flat surface. One way is not necessarily more difficult than the other, but they are different.

The choice of media rests with you, and you will soon learn that the rough sketch on a sheet of paper is only the beginning. The final satisfactory result will be achieved only after numerous trials. This applies equally to advance students or professionals and beginners.

The person with limited experience thinks that he is the only one for whom things don't always turn out as he imagines them or would like to see them. It ought to be both a consolation and an impetus to the student to know that no one, however skillful, is ever really satisfied with most of the work he turns out. Remember, when things don't go right, and you are having a lot of trouble with your design, the other fellow is going through the same torture.

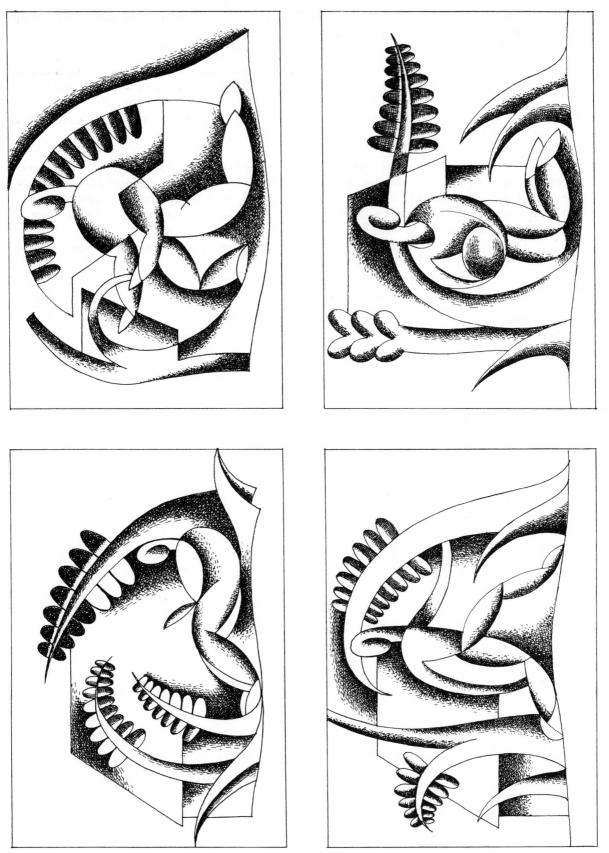

PLATE 10

P L A T E   11.   This plate shows free-form interpretations of the human figure combined within given areas to form compositions.

E X E R C I S E S :

(1) Start with a definite subject in mind, such as dancing, for example, and draw as many skeletal figures as you can (Plate 1A). Then transform into free-form figures (Plate 1D).

(2) Combine into groups of two or more. Keep in mind the extreme contour. (Plate 3.)

The free forms shown in Plate 11 offer a comparatively simple way to use the human figure. They allow much more freedom of expression, particularly for those who have had little or no training and experience in drawing than would otherwise be possible. It would be a mistake for you to infer from the above statement that, if you cannot draw, no effort beyond that of using the free form should be made.

Drawing is the foundation of all creative expression in art. I cannot conceive of anyone, past or present, who has done too much of it.

PLATE 11

PLATE 12. The illustrations in Plate 12 show three-dimensional interpretations of the human form in which ribbon-like surfaces play an important part.

The surfaces are plane, cylindric, twisted cylindric, and modified spherical.

EXERCISES:

    (1) Start with a thin, rectangular block.
        (Use paper if you have nothing else)

    (2) Cut out the simplified, human shape.

    (3) This step involves shaping, indenting, twisting to give the required action and three-dimensional quality and balance necessary for the design.

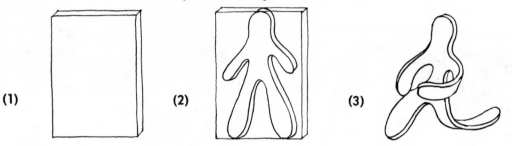

(1)   (2)   (3)

NOTE: See plates on various types of surfaces and solids in chapter on Geometric form.

A study of cylindric surfaces will be of special importance in connection with work of this type.

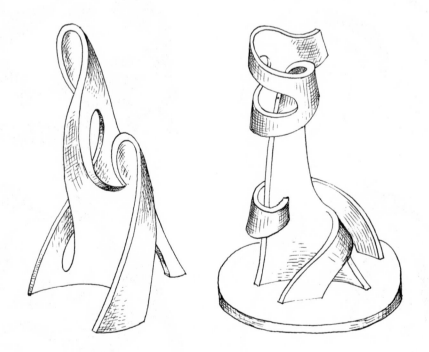

PLATE 12

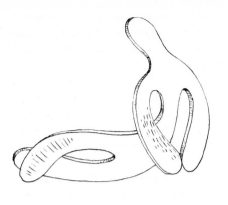
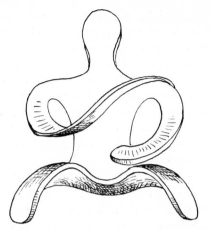
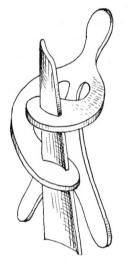
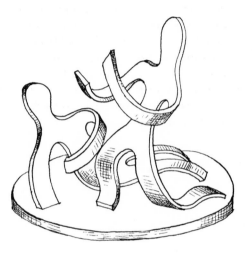
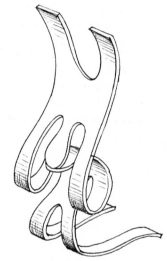
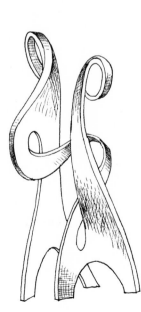
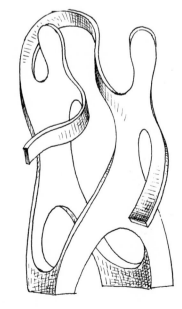
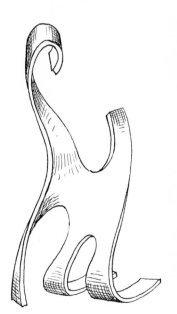

P L A T E 12, continued

P L A T E   13 .   The group of nine illustrations in Plate 13, based on the human figure, may be used both two and three-dimensionally. Treated as two-dimensional figures, they
may be painted, drawn, or etched on surfaces such as paper, canvas, clay or metal. The complexity of the figures does not interfere too much with its execution. It is principally a question
of taking care that the drawing follows the design.

When the figures in Plate 13 are to be transformed into three dimensions, the problems
of construction and medium play a major role. The physical problem of creating something into
a sculptural form is almost always a more difficult one than doing something two-dimensionally .

This does not mean that two-dimensional design conception is less difficult than
volume design. It means that the two types of design are different and call for different frames
of thinking.

Design and the medium in which the design is made go hand-in-hand. Generally speaking, a design is not an all-purpose arrangement suitable for any medium without modification.
The ceramist must think in terms of a medium which is handled differently, which behaves
differently, and whose final product is different from that of a silversmith. Each craftsman
will take into account the problems peculiar to his medium and his way of working, and the
designs created under these conditions will reflect the medium and the personality behind it.

The beginner, whether he is a painter in oil or water-color, a sculptor in wood or stone,
a craftsman in metal or clay, tends to separate the problems of design and the problems of
execution. As experience and confidence are gained, the two problems are joined until a point
is reached when the design and the medium are associated.

We are apt to say that it is a natural thing for a ceramist to think in terms of his material,
clay. It isn't natural at all. It comes only after long experience and conscious effort. This
applies equally well to all other forms of creative art.

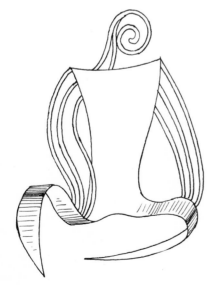
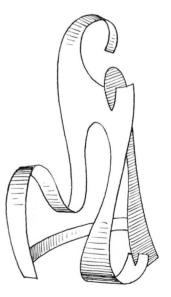

P L A T E   13

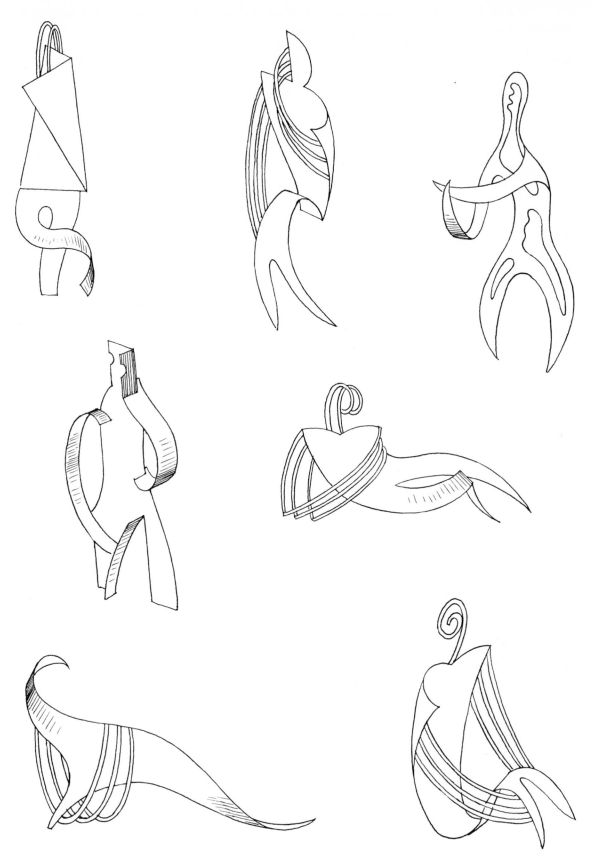

PLATE 13, continued

PLATE 14. Composition 1 in Plate 14 represents a circus. The figures are free-form and represent a wide variety of action.

It is worth repeating that the free-form figure is comparatively easy to handle and makes any composition involving the representation of the human figure a less formidable task.

The composition in 1 is basically radial. Both the linear action and the distribution of lights and darks tend to converge toward an area near the top of the design.

1.

Example 2 represents a group of basketball players. The essential design in this composition is composed of groups of converging lines.

2.

As has been suggested in other parts of this book, one of the easiest ways to start a composition is to select a definite subject, preferably one in which the figures suggest a great deal of physical motion. The feeling of motion will suggest itself in rythmic lines that will add life to the design.

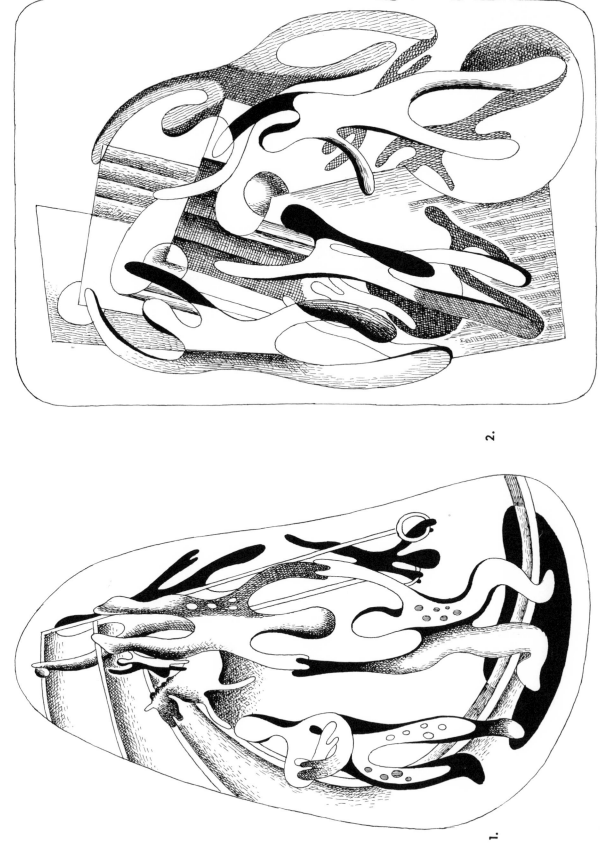

2.

1.

PLATE 14

SECTION SIX

COMPOSITION

INTRODUCTION

Composition as defined in Webster's dictionary, is the 'art or practice of so combining the parts of a work of art as to produce a harmonious whole'. As used in the following pages, the word will, of course, be limited to the graphic arts.

A composition is the result of the act of invention and production.

Designers, painters, sculptors, and craftsmen work with line, color, stone, wood, metal, linen, wool, and a host of other materials to give tangible and visible form to their designs or inventions.

We are perfectly aware of the fact that a straight line can be drawn in a vast number of positions upon a sheet of paper that is limited in size and shape. Each different position of the line means a different arrangement. As we add other lines, not necessarily straight, the number of possible combinations increases considerably. If we introduce color, along with what we already have, there is no end to the variations of different arrangements into which our sheet of paper may be divided. If we are working with wood, stone, or metals of various kinds, and are thinking and inventing spatially or in three dimensions, we become aware of the limitless ways in which our designs can take shape.

One of the first things that the student of design and composition discovers is that, even if he works with what may be regarded as simple or meager source material, there are endless design possibilities present, and that only the limited capacity for invention stands in the way of the designer.

The endless ways in which surfaces and solids can be subdivided, or in which the shapes of three-dimensional objects may be changed by the addition of new spatial objects, pose a problem for the creator. He must come to a decision regarding his choice of subject matter. He must decide on the technique, the material, the size, and the design. All the factors that go into the final decision have not been enumerated, but enough of them have been mentioned to emphasize the point that control is of the utmost necessity.

Sometimes the creator may have no choice as to subject matter, size, or physical material with which the work is to be done. The one area in which there is the greatest freedom is that of arrangement or composition. Even if some restrictions are imposed, there remains such a great latitude for invention that the restrictions cannot be regarded as serious handicaps to the designer.

The need for order is paramount if the final product is to have any meaning to anyone other than the creator. If the designer lives in a vacuum, that is one thing, but such a case would be rare indeed. The artist lives in a world in which he is sensitive, not only to form and color, but to ideas and to the way people react to ideas. These things help to influence and define the artistic products at any given period. This is not to say that every fleeting notion that happens to be in vogue at the moment so influences the creator that his work is immediately affected by it. If this were true, the artist would be at the mercy of all the currents and cross-currents that are ever present.

The creator does have a choice and in his work, if nowhere else, creates a kind of order that is consistent with his ideas.

The basic or fundamental variations of order or composition are quite limited. The multitude of different arrangements are more a matter of degree than of kind.

There is one primary difference between two-dimensional and three-dimensional design that is of great importance to us. Obviously a three-dimensional object must have depth. A two-dimensional arrangement gives the illusion of depth.

Strictly speaking, there is no such thing as flat design in which there is absolutely no sense of depth. It is a matter of degree only. The illusion of depth can be achieved in many ways, and it is one of the factors which the designer must take into account.

Tension is another attribute of composition that plays an important part in creating design. In recent years, the term has gained wide acceptance and at times is used with reckless abandon. A force acting in tension tends to pull things apart. This tendency creates in design a feeling of motion. It must be controlled. Otherwise, it will tend to divide an arrangement into conflicting parts. Unless the conflict is resolved, we have areas vying for attention that confuse the composition as a whole.

Tension is a matter of degree just as is the illusion of depth. Every composition has it to a limited extent. An awareness of its presence is important to the designer.

Throughout this book I have used on numerous occasions the terms 'design ' and 'composition' interchangeably. There is no great difference between them. Perhaps the only difference is that   composition is a more inclusive term embracing design.

P L A T E   1.   The illustrations show various examples of movement by radiation . Radiation implies a source from which all lines emerge or toward which all lines seem to flow.

E X A M P L E S :   'A', 'N', 'O', show how movement is controlled towards a focal point or area.

E X A M P L E S :   'E', 'G', illustrate how the motion seems to emerge from a central point or area.

E X A M P L E S :   'C' and 'L' show, by controlled motion, how there may be more than one focal point or area. This sets up tensions which add a more lively quality to the design. However, care must be taken to make one of the focal areas the unmistakable chief interest.

Every arrangement must be composed of various parts which differ in their importance. If all the components are of equal value, each of them is vying for equal attention, and the result is confusion.

A good rule to follow is to decide on the location of the area of chief interest and then to keep it constantly in mind as the design grows and becomes more involved.

P R O B L E M :   (1) Analyze the examples shown. Look for (a) Essential movement; (b) Tensions; (c) Variations.

> (2) Create series of radial designs showing:
>> (a) 1 focal area
>> (b) 2 focal areas
>> (c) 3 focal areas
>> (d) 4 focal areas

(N O T E :   Be sure that one of the focal areas is the area of chief interest and the others of lesser importance. The lesser focal areas must balance each other.)

E X A M P L E :   Problem 2(c)

E X A M P L E :   Problem 2(d)

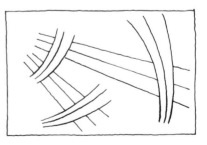

PLATE 1

PLATE 2. Dominant and sub-dominant areas.

Since every composition contains areas that differ in shape and size, it is necessary to establish their relative importance. The first principle that guides us states that all parts of a design are not of equal importance. Keeping this in mind, we must decide which area is to be most important. The most important or dominant space will contain the area of chief interest, (center of interest). Then in the order of their importance, come the sub-dominant areas. There may be many sub-dominant areas depending upon the complexity of the design.

The importance of control cannot be overemphasized. This applies to every minute portion of the work. As has been pointed out before, there is no unimportant part of a composition. Complete mastery implies complete control. Very often sub-dominant or background areas are left to shift for themselves and they become an afterthought. When this happens, the sub-dominant spaces are never fully integrated in the design. When this occurs, it indicates a lack of control on the part of the designer. Luck or chance then enter the picture. At best it is a poor substitute for careful study, sensitivity, and a working knowledge of the general principles that govern the creation of any art work.

E X E R C I S E :

       (1)   Analyze the compositions in Plate 2 and other plates.

       (2)   Study the works of both the past masters and contemporary creators. (Do not copy them. Discover the schematic devices used).

       (3)   Choose a subject that interests you and create a series of layouts, sketchy in effect, which form the basis for further development.

B

A

PLATE 2

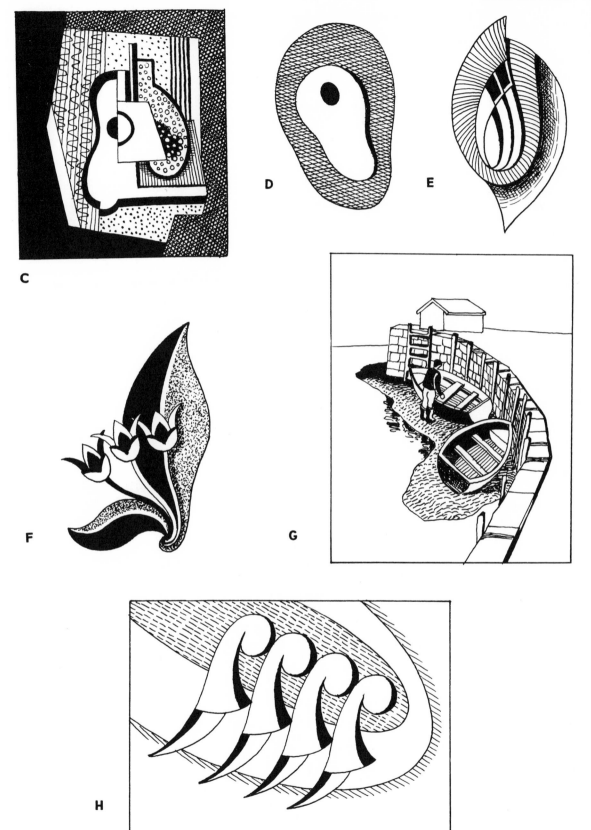

C

D

E

F

G

H

PLATE 2, *continued*

P L A T E 3.   Application of radiation and variants.

Linear analysis of:

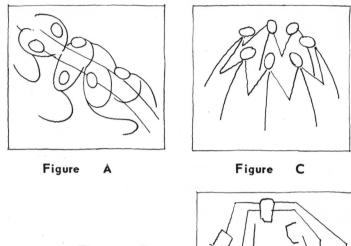

Figure   A   Figure   C

Figure   F

A linear analysis of a composition which has been rendered in a wide range of values or color gives us only a partial breakdown of the essential structure of the work. Its importance lies in the fact that, with rare exceptions, every composition has a beginning in line, in which the designer tries to work out the general movement, establish the area of chief interest, and introduce the balancing subordinate parts. This holds true for three-dimensional design as well , whether it be the work of sculptor or craftsman in metal.

Whenever two or more lines meet or appear to meet, a focal point or area comes into existence which arrests the attention. Almost every composition is made up in part of radial areas.

E X E R C I S E S: Analyze the six compositions in Plate 3.

A. Note the various types of rhythm created by the repetition of almost identical areas.

B. Note the balance of intersecting lines which lie outside the area of chief interest.

C. Note the different directions of motion induced by changes in value, direc-tion, repetition of lines, and areas.

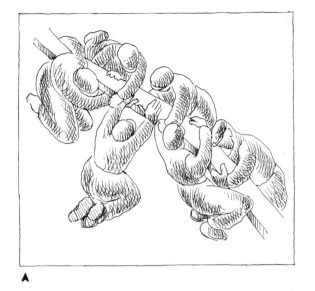

A

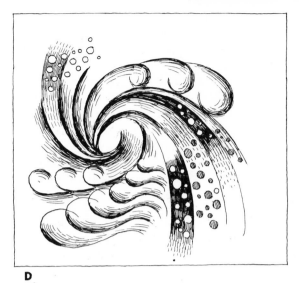

D

B

E

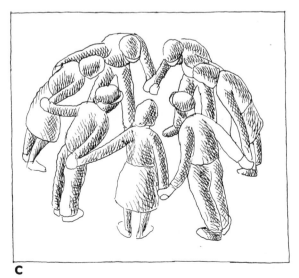

C

F

PLATE 3

P L A T E   4 .   Dominant areas and their control.

Each composition in Plate 4 shows a combination of a dominant and a sub-dominant area. Each area is partially complete with its own focal spot, but the greater emphasis is given to the dominant space. The dominant and sub-dominant areas are united to relieve the tension which arises when two or more elements exist in the same composition.

The two major divisions of each arrangement have many differences, but there is enough of common interest that tends to unite them.

While variety is a highly desirable attribute, there can be too much of it, and too much of it leads to confusion.

There is a vast difference between (1) a lively interplay of varying lines, plane areas, surfaces and color that are controlled and (2) a conglomeration of differing motifs that make up a composition but are in no way connected.

E X E R C I S E: (1) Examine the way in which the parts of each composition are united.
(2) Separate the dominant and sub-dominant areas, and analyze each.
(3) Create a series of compositions of two and three major divisions.

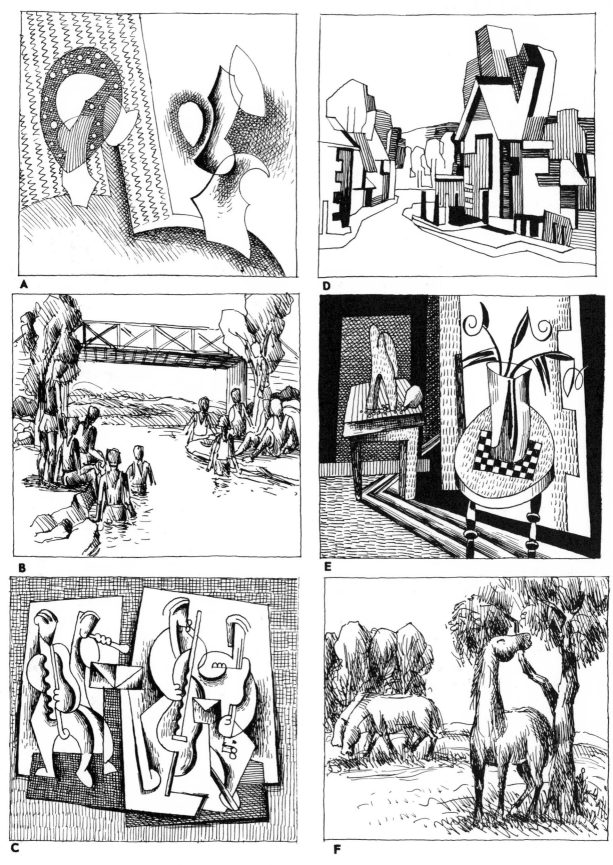

PLATE 4

P L A T E 5 . Compositions using triangular shapes.

Plate 5 shows six examples of the use of the triangle and its variants as a basic shape in composition.

N O T E :   The three-dimensional equivalent of the triangle is the pyramid. All lateral sides of a pyramid are triangles and the lateral edges meet in a common point, the apex. (See Plate 17, Geometric form.)

The triangle is an extremely useful geometric shape that finds frequent use by artists, sculptors, craftsmen, and designers in general. Its general use may be ascribed to the fact that the triangle is the simplest of all closed shapes, having variety in contour and direction of sides. Furthermore, the converging sides offer points or areas of interest which help establish dominant spots.

In the six examples shown, the basic triangular shapes occur most often but are not used exclusively. It would be quite possible to design each closed area of a composition so that the general triangle is the only shape used. The inherent danger in so much repetition may be a dulness that comes from too much sameness. The exclusive use of a single shape is a rarity, but the use of a dominant shape, as illustrated in Plate 5, is not uncommon.

As an exercise in invention, the use of a repeated simple shape, not necessarily a triangle, offers interesting possibilities for creating new combinations of lines, areas, and volumes.

6 A

Whether the use of a basic triangular shape or any other basic shape will adequately express the mood and emotion that the designer wants to reveal is quite another matter. Sometimes the selection of a motif is intuitive, but most often it is chosen because experience prompts the choice.

The subject matter in illustrations 6A and 6B is the same as that of number 6 in Plate 5.

The dominant basic figure in 6A is a quadrilateral, a four-sided figure, and in 6B a free-form, modified ellipse.

The extreme contours suggest triangulation, just as in all of the examples in Plate 5. The internal areas are quite different due to the difference in shape between the triangle, the quadrilateral and the modified ellipse.

6 B

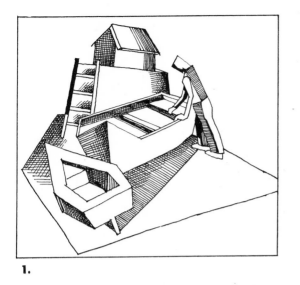

1.

2.

3.

4.

5.

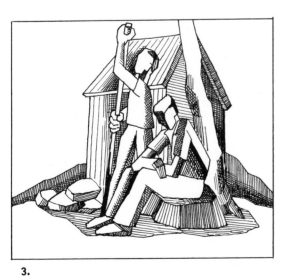

6.

PLATE 5

P L A T E 6. **Variations based on figure group.**

Three-dimensional interpretations of the source material in Plate 6.

Fig. 1 is a composition using metal as a medium.

1.

Fig. 2 is a composition using clay as a medium.

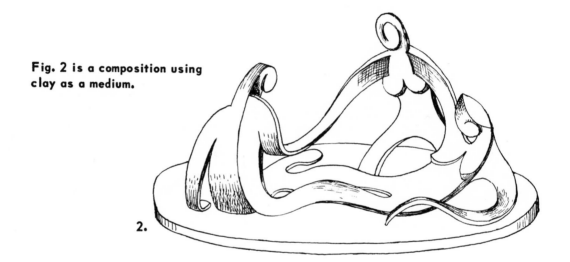

2.

Fig. 3 is a composition using basic triangle and variants as suggested by source material, in Plate 6.

3.

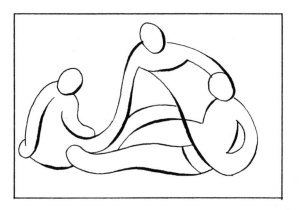
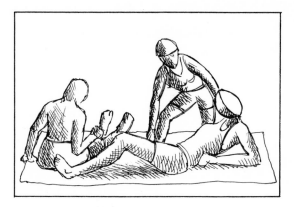
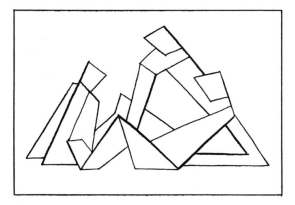

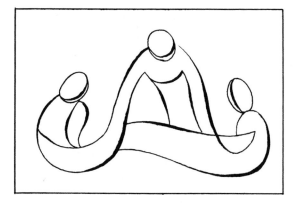
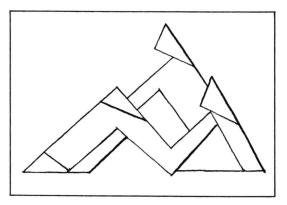

PLATE 6

PLATE 7. Changes in emphasis in composition.

The original sketch for this plate was made in Gloucester, Mass. some years ago. It has been used as basic material for many different pictures that were painted in oil and water-color.

Figure A is a first variation of the original sketch retaining a considerable amount of realism.

Figure 1 is the linear stylization in which the arcs of the elliptical contour are repeated in the figures. The same linear arrangement is used in each of the other compositions.

The essential difference between Figures 2, 3, 4, and 5, is in the change in location of area of chief interest in each composition.

EXERCISE: Use Figs. a, b, c. Create several variations in light and dark values. In each case change the focal area.

a.

b.

c.

A

1.

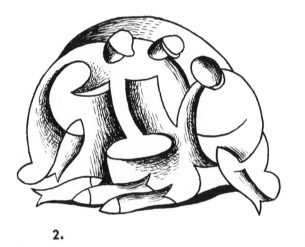

2.

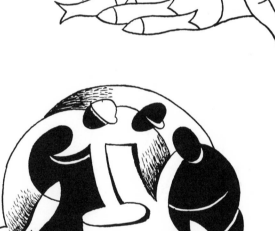

3.

4.

5.

PLATE 7

P L A T E   8 .   Variations using one basic figure.

In Plate 8, Figure A has been used as the central figure in each of the five compositions. It illustrates how the character of the figures changes somewhat as the neighboring lines and shapes change. It would be equally true if the setting were fixed and the figures changed. It is important to realize that only in theory do lines, shapes, volumes, and color exist as separate entities and can be so regarded without reference to any setting or neighbor.

As soon as we put down two or more lines, two or more colors, each one is to some degree affected by the others. This is why it is necessary to experiment. The more of it we do, the more closely will the finished work approximate the imagined one.

We know how often, after a job is done, how far we have strayed from the concept which fired our imagination and impelled us to turn out the painting, the piece of sculpture, the bowl, or whatever else prompted us to creative effort.

The great amount of control and discipline that is necessary in order to achieve anything resembling the idea calls for continued experiments.

It is well to add a word of warning at this point. The compositions in Plate 8 are not intended to show that any setting will go with the basic figure. The illustrations are not offered as a pill that cures everything. They are used to show:

(1) Varied interests can be widely used.
(2) Greater selection is possible with diverse interests.
(3) The inter-dependence of the various parts of a design.
(4) Need for experimentation.

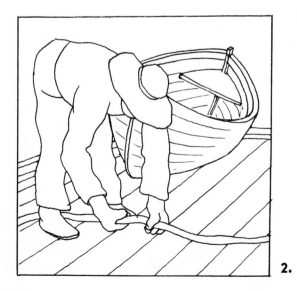

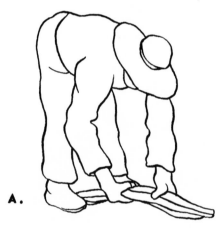

A.

1.

2.

P L A T E   8

3.

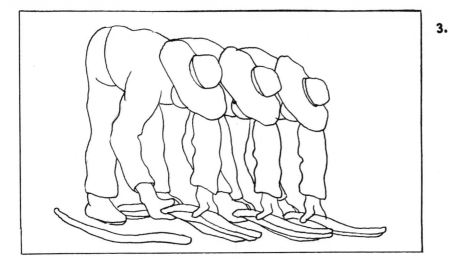

4.

5.

PLATE 8, continued

P L A T E   9 .   Rhythms based on horizontal and vertical lines.

When two lines intersect, the point at which they meet becomes a focal point and claims our attention. In most compositions, there are many focal points because there are many combinations of lines that intersect.

One of the important problems that a designer must recognize and cope with is the control of focal points of intersection so that they create a sense of order. (In three-dimensional design, the problem is further complicated by focal lines which are the intersections between surfaces).

The four illustrations in Plate 9 show different rhythms and space emphases. Each is produced by the intersection of horizontal and vertical lines. The horizontal and vertical lines were selected because they are constantly before us as we view man-made interiors and buildings.

The four compositions suggest, more or less, groups of buildings, but the use of horizontal and vertical lines need not be so limited. When we use slanting lines exclusively, we have greater freedom of expression. We do not have to resort to parallelism as we must when only horizontals and verticals are used. (All vertical lines must be parallel to each other, and all horizontal lines must be parallel to each other when they are shown in the same two-dimensional composition. However, all slanting lines need not be parallel to each other because the angles of slope may vary.)

The greatest freedom of expression comes with the use of the greatest number of different types of lines in combination (straight, curved, vertical, horizontal, slanting, and long and short).

The greatest freedom calls for the greatest amount of control.

E X A M P L E :   Combinations of horizontal and vertical lines that are not suggestive of buildings.

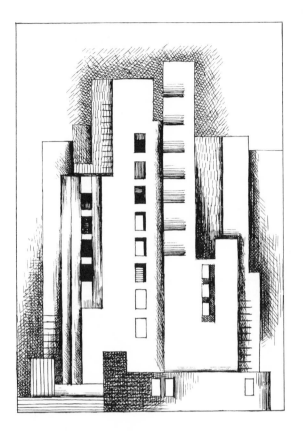

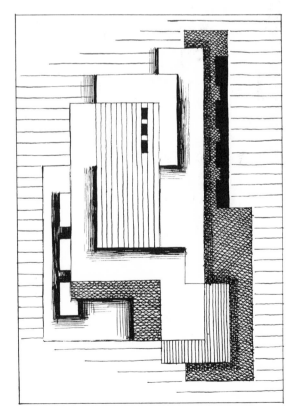

PLATE 9

P L A T E 10. Basic straightline combinations

Plate 10 shows the following basic linear arrangements:

(1)   Dominant   vertical.
(2)   Dominant   diagonal.
(3)   Counterbalancing dominant diagonals.
(4)   Dominant parallel verticals and counterbalancing horizontals.
(5)   Dominant vertical and dominant diagonal.
(6)   Dominant parallel verticals and counterbalancing diagonal.
(7)   Dominant counterbalancing parallel diagonals.
(8)   Dominant parallel horizontals and counterbalancing verticals.
(9)   Dominant diagonal and counterbalancing horizontal.

The illustrations below emphasize the same basic combinations as in Plate 10.

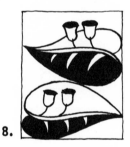

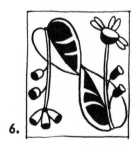

1.

2.

3.

4.

5.

6.

7.

8.

9.

1.

2.

3.

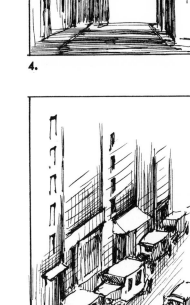

4.

5.

6.

7.

8.

9.

PLATE 10

PLATE 11. Different views of sculptural figures.

In Plate 11, A shows three views of a composition involving three figures. These are drawings made from the actual ceramic piece that I created several years ago.

The middle or front view is intended to be the most important. In dealing with sculptural form, it is not always easy to talk of a chief point of view and subordinate points of view. This is because the piece may be viewed from many different points, and each view should hold our interest.

The first question that arises is whether there should or should not be equal interest from all points of view. The second question is whether it is possible to design three-dimensionally so that all points of view will be of equal importance.

Theoretically, it may be possible to create a form that holds equal interest from all points of view, but actually it is a rare occurrence. In actual practice, the three-dimensional designer aspires to achieve over-all interest and interest in each part, but because he conceives his work with certain definite emphases, he concentrates on them and assigns to these centers the attention that will give them more importance. Such a procedure does not mean that any part is neglected and left to shift for itself. The natural approach, or at least the most common approach, in all forms of creative work is to conceive and design climaxes that are reached in a controlled way. The climaxes in art are the areas of chief interest.

Figure B in Plate 11 is much more abstract in feeling and delineation than Figure A. That does not make it better or worse than Figure A. It just makes it different.

As we depart more and more from realism, we come closer to the point where it may be possible to create sculpturally something that may be viewed from every point of view with equal interest.

This has nothing to do with the value of the work as an art form. The degree of abstraction of a creation does not determine its excellence.

Fig. A

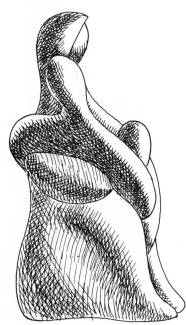
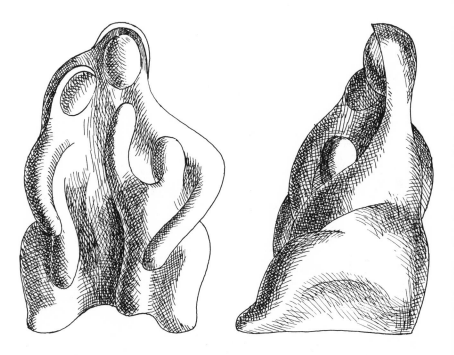

PLATE 11

Fig. B

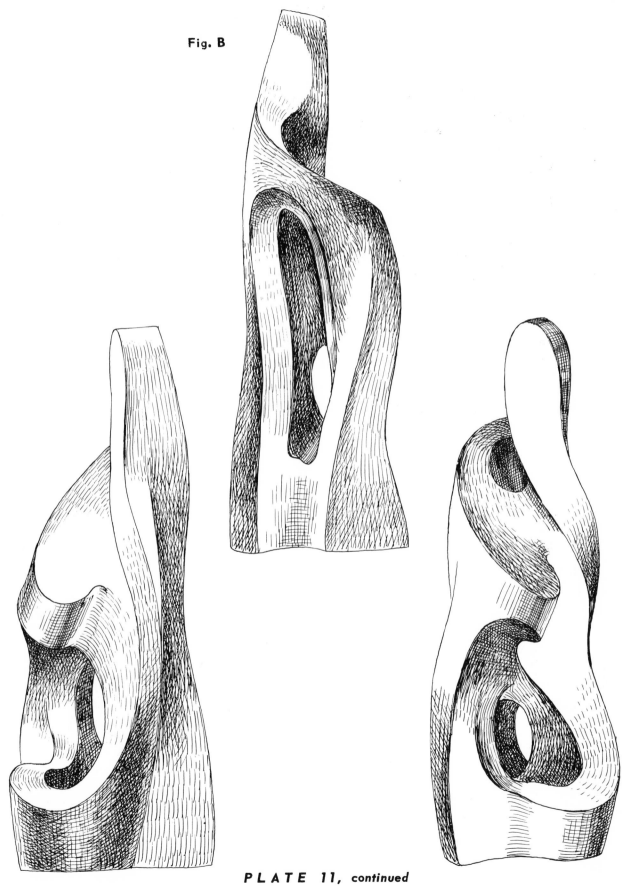

PLATE 11, continued